# AWS Networking Cookbook

Powerful recipes to overcome the pain points of optimizing your Virtual Private Cloud (VPC)

**Satyajit Das**
**Jhalak Modi**

BIRMINGHAM - MUMBAI

# AWS Networking Cookbook

First published: August 2017

Production reference: 1210817

Published by Packt Publishing Ltd.
Livery Place
35 Livery Street
Birmingham
B3 2PB, UK.

ISBN 978-1-78712-324-3

www.packtpub.com

# Credits

**Authors**
Satyajit Das
Jhalak Modi

**Reviewers**
Appasaheb Bagali
Adrin Mukherjee
Legorie Rajan

**Commissioning Editor**
Vijin Boricha

**Acquisition Editor**
Heramb Bhavsar

**Content Development Editor**
Devika Battike

**Technical Editor**
Aditya Khadye

**Copy Editor**
Juliana Nair

**Project Coordinator**
Judie Jose

**Proofreader**
Safis Editing

**Indexer**
Aishwarya Gangawane

**Graphics**
Kirk D'Penha

**Production Coordinator**
Aparna Bhagat

# About the Authors

**Satyajit Das** has more than sixteen years of IT experience. He is currently working as an AWS CoE lead cloud architect in a large enterprise. He has also worked as an enterprise architect, solution architect, and technical architect in recent engagements. He has guided, designed, integrated, implemented, and governed enterprise-grade applications. He works on building solutions using microservices on the hybrid cloud using DevOps principles. He has extensively worked on IoT, AWS, and cloud migration.

Satyajit has worked in leading organizations, such as Wipro, Infosys, PwC, and Accenture, in various challenging roles.

*I would like to thank the extremely helpful and supportive editorial team at Packt, who enabled me to write my first book.*

*I would like to thank the Wipro management team and colleagues for providing support while I was writing this book. I'll take this opportunity to thank Vipul for mentoring and motivating me to take up new challenges and learning opportunity.*

*I would like to thank my entire family, especially my wife, Papiya, for supporting me through all the ups and downs. I would like to dedicate this book to my father, Sasadhar, who guided me and made me who I am today, and my lovely son, Shreyas, to whom I cannot give much time due to the challenges of my professional career.*

**Jhalak Modi** is a DevOps, cloud architect, and an AWS trainer with a deep interest and expertise in implementing multi-tier architectures, cluster platforms, and automation solutions. She is an AWS certified solutions architect professional and a certified DevOps professional with 10+ certifications in trending technologies.

Jhalak is also a public speaker at various AWS events, colleges/universities, and meet-ups, and has provided AWS and Linux training at several renowned institutes and corporates. Currently, she is working with KOGENTiX and has worked with Wipro Technologies and Electromech Corporation in the past.

*I would like to dedicate this book to my parents for always believing in me and loving me unconditionally.*

*Special thanks to my husband, Darshan, for his constant guidance, support, and patience. Without him, this book would be impossible.*

*Many thanks to Karishma Modi, Hardik Modi, and my in-laws; you all mean a lot to me.*

*Many heartfelt thanks and gratitude go out to Vipul Tankariya, Bhavin Parmar, Divya Tiwari, and my co-author, Satyajit Das, and all the mentors (Ashutosh Pancholi, Shivram Meena, Rukhsana Saifee, Anu Badola, Sadhandan PT, Jai Malhotra, and Shiksha Kanwar).*

*Thanks to Packt's Heramb Bhavsar, Devika Battike, and team for putting up with my random schedule and making this a better book with their diligent reviewing efforts.*

*Finally, there would be no book about AWS networking without AWS. I wish to thank the AWS team for their extraordinary documents.*

# About the Reviewers

**Appasaheb Bagali** is an AWS solution architect working with enterprise customers. His love for computers drove him to pursue a master's degree in computer application (MCA) and has not looked back ever since. He started his career as a web developer, and is currently working as an AWS solutions architect and helps customers understand how to transform their IT infrastructure, operations, and applications to make the most of the scalability, innovation, and cost efficiency of the AWS platform. He loves to hack around DevOps and automation using Puppet and AWS CloudFormation.

He lives in Banglore with his wife, Sandhya, and son, Pritam.

**Adrin Mukherjee** is a passionate software engineer and a technical architect with expertise in building distributed applications and high-performance systems. He has 13 years of experience in the IT industry and is presently working as a solution architect at Wipro.

His current focus is on cloud computing, NoSQL, and machine learning.

**Legorie Rajan** is a cloud consultant working with enterprise customers in the banking and insurance domains. He started his career as a mainframe developer and is currently working as a solution architect on the cloud and helps with migration of applications to the cloud. He loves to hack around with new languages; his current side projects use NodeJs, Mongo, and Kubernetes. He has a B.Tech (CS) from Pondicherry University and MS (Mgmt) from Grenoble Graduate School of Business.

He lives in Chennai with his wife, Anitha Sophie, and son, Reuel Bepin.

# www.PacktPub.com

For support files and downloads related to your book, please visit www.PacktPub.com.

Did you know that Packt offers eBook versions of every book published, with PDF and ePub files available? You can upgrade to the eBook version at www.PacktPub.com and as a print book customer, you are entitled to a discount on the eBook copy. Get in touch with us at service@packtpub.com for more details.

At www.PacktPub.com, you can also read a collection of free technical articles, sign up for a range of free newsletters and receive exclusive discounts and offers on Packt books and eBooks.

https://www.packtpub.com/mapt

Get the most in-demand software skills with Mapt. Mapt gives you full access to all Packt books and video courses, as well as industry-leading tools to help you plan your personal development and advance your career.

## Why subscribe?

- Fully searchable across every book published by Packt
- Copy and paste, print, and bookmark content
- On demand and accessible via a web browser

# Customer Feedback

Thanks for purchasing this Packt book. At Packt, quality is at the heart of our editorial process. To help us improve, please leave us an honest review on this book's Amazon page at https://www.amazon.com/dp/1787123243.

If you'd like to join our team of regular reviewers, you can e-mail us at customerreviews@packtpub.com. We award our regular reviewers with free eBooks and videos in exchange for their valuable feedback. Help us be relentless in improving our products!

# Table of Contents

# Preface

There is no debate on the fact that Cloud is going to be the default infrastructure provider as it provides numerous benefits. The most important aspects of cloud computing are as follows:

- Massive scale: This can virtually serve resources for all programming needs to anyone without the need to build a massive scale computing infrastructure
- On demand access: The resources can be provisioned by self-service instantly when required and released when not needed any more

Cloud computing is being used by organizations to do the following:

- Increase agility of the organization through purchase provision deploy and manage applications, services dynamically and secure support in real time based on demand without managing compute, network and other resources
- Cut overall cost of ownership and upfront investment for resources and pay only for the resources being used
- Utilize software tools and services as per the requirement offered by cloud providers instead of purchasing and owning them
- Reduced time to market products and services due to reduced time cycle for accruing infrastructure resources to build and deploy them
- Increase in reliability and availability as cloud providers offer multiple data centers that can be used for disaster recovery options if some data center goes down

That's why organizations are thinking about cloud first approach for hosting their services in cloud. AWS is the most popular public cloud service. It's a challenge for architects and DevOps professionals for building infrastructure in AWS right the first time itself. This book will provide a practical and simple-to-follow approach for creating, managing, and automating AWS networking components. It will also provide insight's best use of different AWS networking services. We'll start simple so that it's easy for first timers. However, we'll dive deep into various AWS networking-related services that are expected out of a seasoned AWS professional.

# What this book covers

Chapter 1, *Getting Started with AWS Networking Components*, helps first timers to create AWS account and users. It guides readers for creating simple AWS networking components from Console and creating first EC2 instance in AWS. It also guides to configure AWS CLI.

Chapter 2, *Building Your Own Custom VPC*, walks through all the necessary steps to different network components in AWS. It guides how to build subnetworks, firewalls, and routing in AWS. It also provides a recipe for creating and connecting to your instance hosted in AWS.

Chapter 3, *VPC Advanced Components*, provides advanced recipes for adding multiple network interfaces to EC2, connecting to Windows and Linux instance. Then it guides to create high available solutions through horizontal scaling using load balancer and launch configuration. It also provides a recipe for connecting multiple VPCs in a region.

Chapter 4, *Configuring Global Scale Infrastructure*, focuses on creating global scale network infrastructure by connecting VPCs across AWS regions or creating a communication channel between VPC and the corporate data center. It also provides a recipe for creating network components from CLI and how to make AWS resources IPv6 compliant.

Chapter 5, *Working with Infrastructure Automation*, provides flexibility to automate network resources such as VPC, subnet, and NAT gateway using Cloudformation and Ansible. Don't worry, this chapter also explains how to set up Cloudformation and Ansible and related playbooks. There are various sample playbooks for you to play with.

Chapter 6, *Working with Route 53*, gives an overall understanding of how DNS works and the different routing policies. This recipe will guide you from buying a domain to creating a highly available DNS routing. This chapter also covers setting up private DNS and monitoring the DNS resources.

Chapter 7, *Cloud Security and Network Compliance*, turns your attention to security. This chapter will help you understand how to prevent and mitigate various attacks such as DDOS and Port scanning using different AWS services (CloudFront, Elastic Load Balancer, Auto Scaling Group, CloudWatch, Trusted Advisor, and CloudTrail)

Chapter 8, *Troubleshooting and VPC Limits*, concentrates various troubleshooting and support issues. It covers most common error messages and configuration problems. The chapter also includes information on how and where you can get support to increase the VPC resource limits

Chapter 9, *Pricing of VPC and Related Components*, guides you to calculate pricing of the infrastructure that you are going to build in AWS.

# What you need for this book

This book assumes basic-level knowledge on Linux operating system and cloud computing. The book will go through building different networking components in AWS, which may require a basic understanding of networking and virtualization concepts. If you have an experience of networking concepts, this is a big plus.

Most of the recipes provided in the book for networking components are provided by AWS and require AWS console access. For this you need moderate network connectivity to the internet. Some of the recipes that are executed on the local system are also very lightweight and can be executed on any laptop or desktop with decent configuration. Sample hardware or virtual requirements are listed as follows:

- CPU: 4 cores
- Memory: 8 GB RAM
- Disk space: 80 GB

In this book, you will need the following software list:

- AWS Tools—AWS CLI
- Putty and puttygen
- Internet Browser
- Ansible
- Python 2.7+
- Pip
- EPEL Repo
- Curl / wget

# Who this book is for

To make use of the content of this book, basic prior knowledge of Cloud and networking is expected. If you do not possess that knowledge, it is always possible to catch up the basic requirements by going through the major components from the AWS documentation at https://aws.amazon.com/documentation/. This covers all the AWS services used in this book and much more. This book is essentially intended to AWS developers, architects, network professionals and DevOps engineers who want a quick start for creating basic infrastructure in the AWS cloud. It will also provide you the steps for creating a global scale production-ready infrastructure using AWS console and Automation tools (CloudFormation and Ansible).

# Sections

In this book, you will find several headings that appear frequently (Getting ready, How to do it..., How it works..., There's more..., and See also). To give clear instructions on how to complete a recipe, we use these sections as follows:

# Getting ready

This section tells you what to expect in the recipe, and describes how to set up any software or any preliminary settings required for the recipe.

# How to do it...

This section contains the steps required to follow the recipe.

# How it works...

This section usually consists of a detailed explanation of what happened in the previous section.

# There's more...

This section consists of additional information about the recipe in order to make the reader more knowledgeable about the recipe.

# See also

This section provides helpful links to other useful information for the recipe.

# Conventions

In this book, you will find a number of text styles that distinguish between different kinds of information. Here are some examples of these styles and an explanation of their meaning.

Code words in text, database table names, folder names, filenames, file extensions, pathnames, dummy URLs, user input, and Twitter handles are shown as follows: "Add `0.0.0.0/0` in the destination."

A block of code is set as follows:

```
#!/bin/bash
yum update -y
yum install -y httpd24 php56 mysql55-server php56-mysqlnd
service httpd start
chkconfig httpd on
groupadd
```

When we wish to draw your attention to a particular part of a code block, the relevant lines or items are set in bold:

```
[root@ansible playbook]# vim awsvpc.yml
---
- name: Create VPC
hosts: localhost
gather_facts: no
roles:
- vpc
```

Any command-line input or output is written as follows:

```
mysql -u root -p
```

**New terms** and **important words** are shown in bold. Words that you see on the screen, for example, in menus or dialog boxes, appear in the text like this: "Click on the button **Create an AWS Account**. "

Warnings or important notes appear like this.

Tips and tricks appear like this.

# Reader feedback

Feedback from our readers is always welcome. Let us know what you think about this book-what you liked or disliked. Reader feedback is important for us as it helps us develop titles that you will really get the most out of. To send us general feedback, simply e-mail feedback@packtpub.com, and mention the book's title in the subject of your message. If there is a topic that you have expertise in and you are interested in either writing or contributing to a book, see our author guide at www.packtpub.com/authors.

# Customer support

Now that you are the proud owner of a Packt book, we have a number of things to help you to get the most from your purchase.

# Downloading the example code

You can download the example code files for this book from your account at http://www.packtpub.com. If you purchased this book elsewhere, you can visit http://www.packtpub.com/support, and register to have the files e-mailed directly to you. You can download the code files by following these steps:

1. Log in or register to our website using your e-mail address and password.
2. Hover the mouse pointer on the **SUPPORT** tab at the top.
3. Click on **Code Downloads & Errata**.
4. Enter the name of the book in the **Search** box.
5. Select the book for which you're looking to download the code files.
6. Choose from the drop-down menu where you purchased this book from.
7. Click on **Code Download**.

You can also download the code files by clicking on the **Code Files** button on the book's webpage at the Packt Publishing website. This page can be accessed by entering the book's name in the **Search** box. Please note that you need to be logged in to your Packt account. Once the file is downloaded, please make sure that you unzip or extract the folder using the latest version of:

- WinRAR / 7-Zip for Windows
- Zipeg / iZip / UnRarX for Mac
- 7-Zip / PeaZip for Linux

The code bundle for the book is also hosted on GitHub at `https://github.com/PacktPublishing/AWS-Networking-Cookbook`. We also have other code bundles from our rich catalog of books and videos available at `https://github.com/PacktPublishing/`. Check them out!

# Downloading the color images of this book

We also provide you with a PDF file that has color images of the screenshots/diagrams used in this book. The color images will help you better understand the changes in the output. You can download this file from `https://www.packtpub.com/sites/default/files/downloads/AWSNetworkingCookbook_ColorImages.pdf`.

# Errata

Although we have taken every care to ensure the accuracy of our content, mistakes do happen. If you find a mistake in one of our books-maybe a mistake in the text or the code-we would be grateful if you could report this to us. By doing so, you can save other readers from frustration and help us improve subsequent versions of this book. If you find any errata, please report them by visiting `http://www.packtpub.com/submit-errata`, selecting your book, clicking on the **Errata Submission Form** link, and entering the details of your errata. Once your errata are verified, your submission will be accepted and the errata will be uploaded to our website or added to any list of existing errata under the Errata section of that title. To view the previously submitted errata, go to `https://www.packtpub.com/books/content/support`, and enter the name of the book in the search field. The required information will appear under the **Errata** section.

# Piracy

Piracy of copyrighted material on the Internet is an ongoing problem across all media. At Packt, we take the protection of our copyright and licenses very seriously. If you come across any illegal copies of our works in any form on the Internet, please provide us with the location address or website name immediately so that we can pursue a remedy. Please contact us at `copyright@packtpub.com` with a link to the suspected pirated material. We appreciate your help in protecting our authors and our ability to bring you valuable content.

# Questions

If you have a problem with any aspect of this book, you can contact us at `questions@packtpub.com`, and we will do our best to address the problem.

# 1
# Getting Started with AWS Networking Components

In this chapter, we'll cover the following recipes:

- Creating an account in AWS
- Creating an admin user in AWS
- Creating a VPC and a subnet with IPv6
- Creating an EC2 with an IPv6 address
- Creating NAT on EC2 instance
- Working with network interfaces
- Configuring AWS CLI

## Introduction

Public cloud computing is a service that can be accessed over the internet. It provides resources, on a shared basis, for hosting applications and data on distributed computing resources. Cloud providers host a pool of services for computer servers, storages, networks, application platforms and software services that are assigned to customers based on their needs. Cloud providers take responsibility of managing computing resources so that customers can concentrate on building applications or services quickly. AWS is the biggest public cloud service provider.

AWS provides most of the networking services that we are going to explore for free. It also lets customers experiment with some of the other services for free at a lower scale. We need to have an account and the required permissions in AWS to execute the recipes provided throughout this book. Creating some of the services may cost some money, so please look into the AWS pricing page (https://aws.amazon.com/pricing/services/) for different services and understand the cost impact that execution of some recipes will have.

# Various AWS network services

In this section, we shall come to understand the building blocks of AWS Cloud. We are going to use or create the following components through this book.

- **Region**: AWS Cloud currently has data centers in 16 cities and is also coming up in new locations throughout the world. Each region is completely isolated from the others. You need to choose one region to create network components.
- **Availability Zone (AZ)**: Each region of AWS Cloud has multiple physically isolated and separate data centers called availability zone. Some network components span across multiple AZs in a region like VPC. Components like subnet are confined within an AZ. AWS provides various networking services as **Platform as a Service (PaaS)**. Examples are:
  - **Route 53**: Distributed, scalable and highly available **Domain Name System (DNS)**
  - **Direct connect**: This provides a dedicated low latency and high bandwidth network connectivity between a data center and an AWS VPC.
  - **ELB**: This is a high availablility and scalable load balancing service provided by AWS.
  - **AWS VPC**: VPC is a virtual network built in the AWS Cloud similar to a network in a data center. It is isolated from other VPCs that are created in your account or other accounts. You can choose the **Classless Inter-Domain Routing** (CIDR) range of the VPC and can create instances with the IP address within that range. **Virtual Routing and Forwarding** (VRF) in conventional networking is equivalent to a VPC in AWS, whereas VLAN is synonymous to a subnet. You can isolate instances in separate VLANs or subnets.

The following figure gives the default VPC components which include **Internet gateway, Virtual private gateway, Router, Route table, Subnet, Network ACL** and **Security group**.

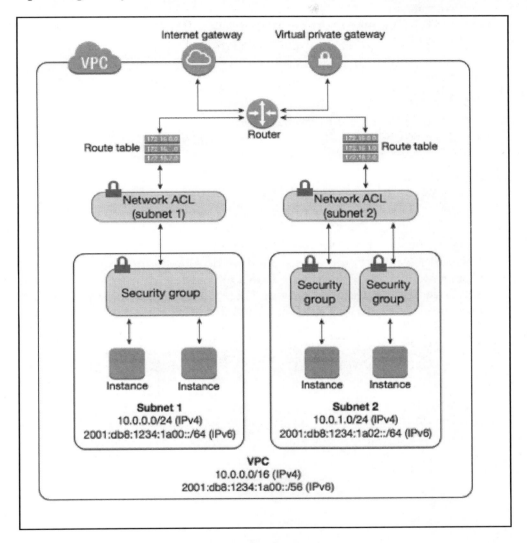

AWS VPC high level components

**Source:** http://docs.aws.amazon.com/AmazonVPC/latest/UserGuide/images/security-diagram.png

# Creating an account in AWS

We are going to create an AWS account in this section. Please skip this section if you already have an AWS account. Otherwise, please follow the step by step process to create an account with AWS.

## Getting ready

Be ready with your credit card information.

## How to do it...

1. Please open the URL https://aws.amazon.com/account/ in your favorite browser.
2. Click on the button **Create an AWS Account**.
3. You will see a page which looks like the following figure. Provide your email or mobile number, select the option **I am a new user** and click on **Sign in using our secure server**. The email ID provided here will be treated as the owner or root user for this account and has exclusive rights to do anything in the account.

Create account--Provide mail or mobile

4.  You will get a page like this. Provide the required details and click on **Create account**.

Create account--Provide personal details

5. Provide additional details for your account.

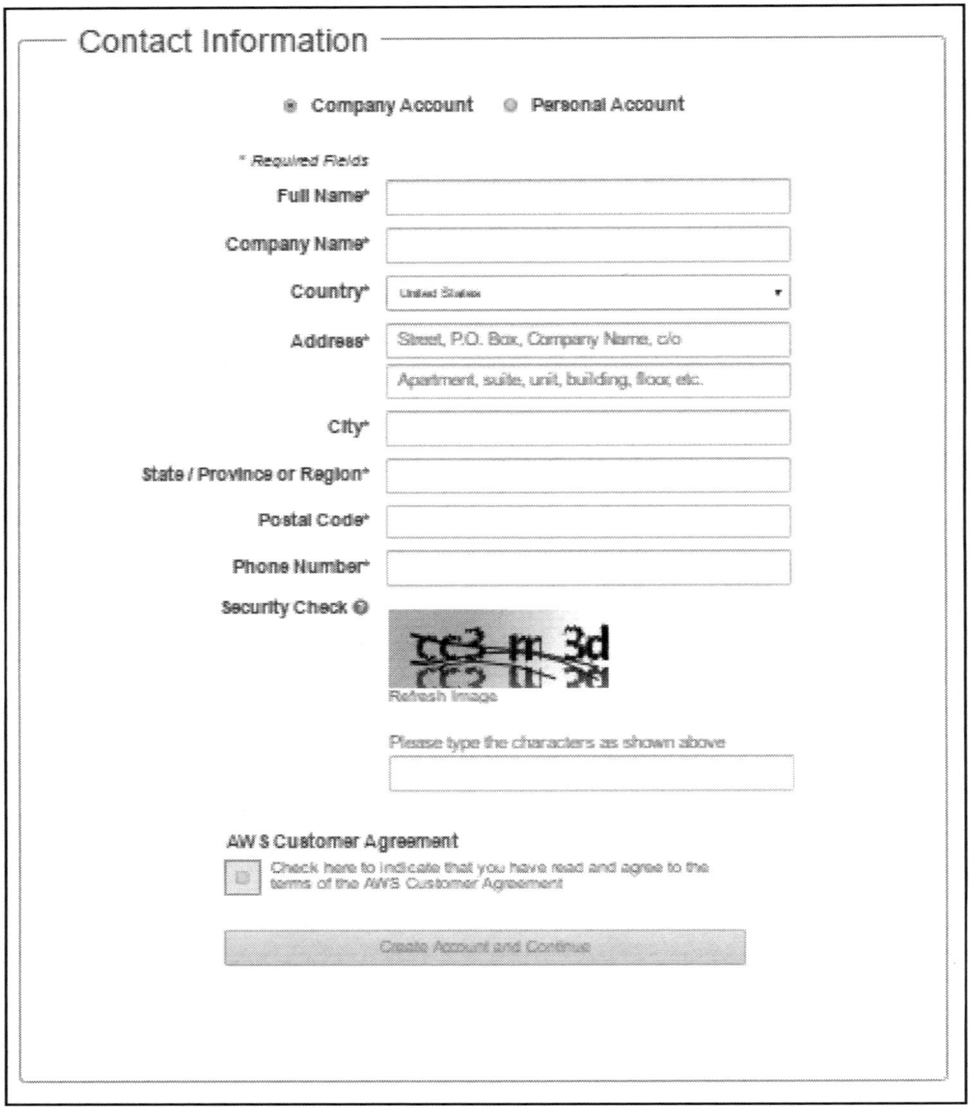

### Contact Information

○ Company Account    ○ Personal Account

\* *Required Fields*

| | |
|---|---|
| **Full Name\*** | |
| **Company Name\*** | |
| **Country\*** | United States ▼ |
| **Address\*** | Street, P.O. Box, Company Name, c/o |
| | Apartment, suite, unit, building, floor, etc. |
| **City\*** | |
| **State / Province or Region\*** | |
| **Postal Code\*** | |
| **Phone Number\*** | |

**Security Check** ◎

```
cc3 m 3d
```

Refresh Image

Please type the characters as shown above

**AWS Customer Agreement**

☐ Check here to indicate that you have read and agree to the terms of the AWS Customer Agreement

Create Account and Continue

Create account--Provide contact information

6. Provide payment information for billing purposes.

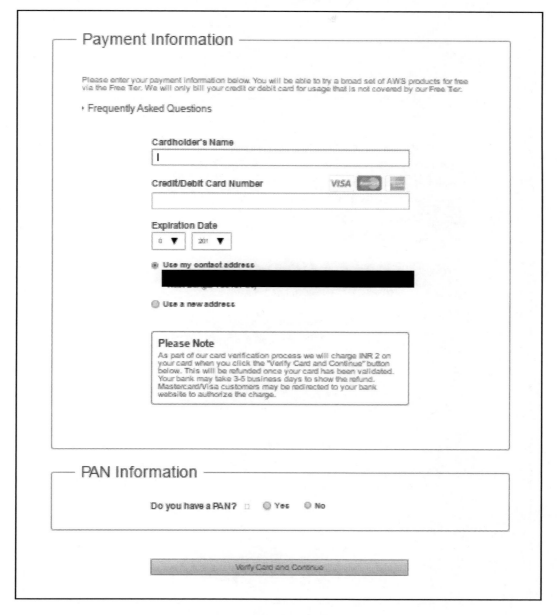

Create account--Provide payment information

7. Provide identity verification. There will be an automated call initiated by AWS to your phone number and you will need to key in the verification code shown on the screen.

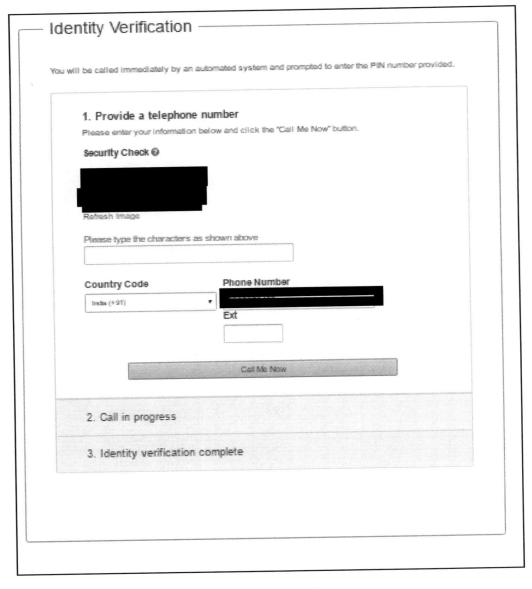

Create account--provide identity verification

8. Choose **Support Plan** and click on **Continue**.

---

## Support Plan

AWS Support offers a selection of plans to meet your needs. All plans provide 24x7 access to customer service, AWS documentation, whitepapers, and support forums. For access to technical support and additional resources to help you plan, deploy, and optimize your AWS environment, we recommend selecting a support plan that best aligns with your AWS usage.

All customers receive free Basic Support.

### Basic Support

● **Basic**

Description: Customer Service for account and billing questions and access to the AWS Community Forums.

Price: Included

○ **Developer**

Use case: Experimenting with AWS

Description: One primary contact may ask technical questions through Support Center and get a response within 12–24 hours during local business hours.

Price: Starts at $29/month (scales based on usage)

○ **Business**

Use case: Production use of AWS

Description: 24x7 support by phone and chat, 1-hour response to urgent support cases, and help with common third-party software. Full access to AWS Trusted Advisor for optimizing your AWS infrastructure, and access to the AWS Support API for automating your support cases and retrieving Trusted Advisor results.

Price: Starts at $100/month (scales based on usage)

To explore all features and benefits of AWS Support, including plan comparisons and pricing samples, click here.

[ Continue ]

Create account–Choose support plan

9. You will see a welcome screen and can log in to the AWS console by clicking on **Sign In to the Console**. You'll also receive an email confirmation for the account creation.

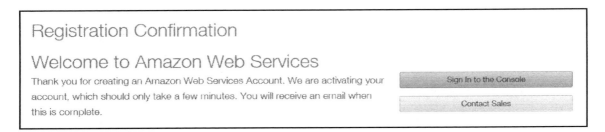

Create account--Registration confirmation

10. After login, you will see a screen like the following:

AWS dashboard

# There's more...

Once you decide to delete your account, you can do so by logging in to your account; see the following figure:

▾ Close Account

☑ I understand that by clicking this checkbox, I am willing to close my AWS account. Monthly usage of certain AWS services is calculated and billed at the beginning of the following month. If you have used these types of services this month, then at the beginning of next month you will receive a bill for usage that occurred prior to termination of your account. If you own a Reserved Instance for which you have elected to pay in monthly installments, when your account is closed you will continue to be billed your monthly recurring payment until the Reserved Instance is sold on the Reserved Instance Marketplace or it expires.

**Close Account**

Delete account

# Creating an admin user in AWS

Once the account is created, we should not use it for anything apart from creating an admin user and handling billing related information. A strong password policy and **multi-factor authentication (MFA)** should be configured for all powerful users. We shall go through the steps to create an admin user. We shall use this user credential for executing recipes for different network elements in AWS. More stringent processes and methods should be followed for creating and managing users in AWS for production purposes.

## Getting ready

Log in to the AWS account with user credentials.

## How to do it...

1. Select **Identity and Access Management (IAM)** service from the console by typing `https://console.aws.amazon.com/iam/` in the browser. You will see the URL that the user other than the root user will need to use for console access.

IAM users sign-in link:

https://███████████.signin.aws.amazon.com/console

URL for AWS console login URL

2. Click on **Users** in the left menu and then click on **Add user**.

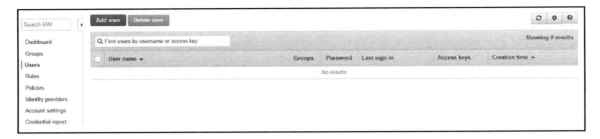

User dashboard

3. Provide a username of your choice. Opt for both programmatic and console access. Select other relevant options and click on **Next: Permission**.

Add user in IAM

4. Choose the option **Attach existing policies directly**. Choose
**AdministratorAccess** and then click **Next: Review**.

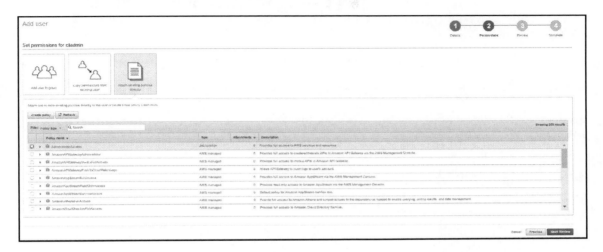

Choose permission

5. Review the details and click on **Create User**.

Review create user

6. Download and store the .csv file in a safe place. The file contains user access
key details and console login link. User access information is required for AWS
service access through program or CLI. It will be used in the later part of the
book.

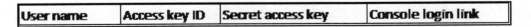

| User name | Access key ID | Secret access key | Console login link |
|-----------|---------------|-------------------|--------------------|

User access key details

# There's more...

The user access details can be used for accessing AWS from **Command Line Interface (CLI)**. Scripts can be written using CLI and can be used as code for managing AWS infrastructure.

# Creating a VPC and a subnet with IPv6

In this section, we shall be creating a VPC and a subnet using wizard to get started quickly.

## Getting ready

We need an AWS account and a user with the proper permissions for creating a VPC and a subnet.

## How to do it...

1. Log in to your AWS account. Select **VPC** in AWS services as shown in the following figure:

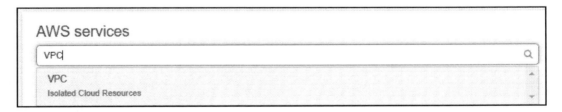

Select VPC from AWS console

2. Click on **Start VPC Wizard**.

VPC dashboard

3. VPC wizard will appear with four options. Now, we shall choose the first one to create our first VPC and subnet. Click on the **Select** button.

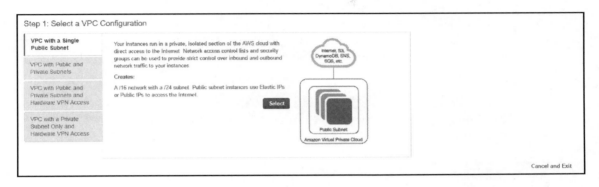

VPC Wizard

4. We need to choose **Amazon provided IPv6 CIDR block** to enable IPv6 for VPC. For a subnet in a drop-down menu **Public subnet's IPv6 CIDR:** we need to select **Specify a custom IPv6 CIDR**. Key in the VPC and subnet names. Keep other options unchanged. Click on th **Create VPC** button.

Create VPC and subnet with IPv6

5. A success message will be displayed as following:

VPC and subnet creation success message

6. Click on **Your VPCs** in the left menu. The VPC will be displayed. If you choose to see details, you can see that a **Network ACL** and **Route table** has been automatically created.

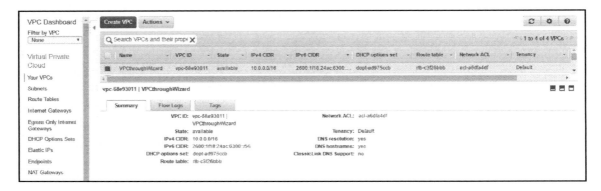

Summary of VPC created

7. Click on **Subnets** on the left menu bar. You will be able to see the subnet that was just created. If you choose to see details, you can see that a **Network ACL** and **Route table** that is automatically created.

Summary of subnet created

8. Click on the **Route Table** tab. You can see that the Route Table includes four entries. Two for internal IPv4 and IPv6 communication and two internet gateways (starting with **igw**) for communication with the outside world for IPv4 and IPv6.

Route Table of subnet created

9. Click on the **Network ACL** tab. You can see that all traffic for both IPv4 and IPv6 has been allowed. We shall learn how to configure the rules in the later section of the book.

Network ACL of subnet created

# Creating an EC2 with an IPv6 address

In this section, we shall be creating an EC2 instance with an IPv6 address in the VPC and subnet that we created using the wizard. EC2 is a virtual machine in AWS that comes as an IaaS offering. You can choose different virtual machine images called **Amazon Machine Image (AMI)** or create your own custom AMI for creating an EC2 instance. We shall also install a web server to test if our steps are correct.

# Getting ready

We need an AWS account and user with proper permissions for creating an EC2 instance.

# How to do it...

1. Log in to your AWS account. Select **EC2** services as shown in the following figure:

Select EC2 service

2. The EC2 dashboard will appear. Click on **Launch Instance** in the EC2 dashboard.

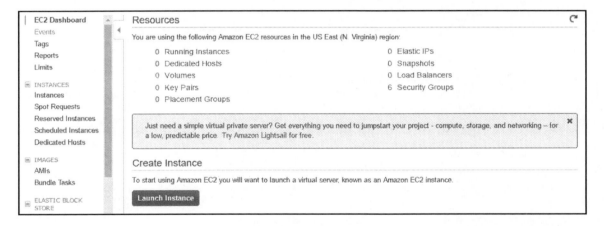

EC2 dashboard

3. Select **Amazon Linux AMI**, which is available on the top of the list

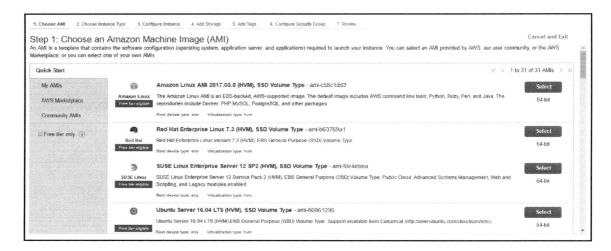

Choose AMI

4. There are many instance types available with different vCPU and memory options. We shall choose **t2.micro** and then click on **Next: Configure Instance Details**.

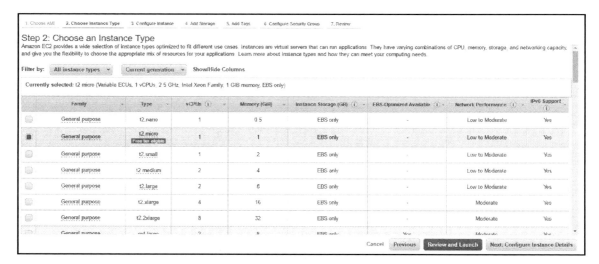

Choose instance type

5. In **Network**, choose the VPC we just created. In **Subnet**, select the subnet we created. In **Auto-assign Public IP**, choose **Enable**. In **Auto-assign IPv6 IP**, choose **Enable**. Click on **Next: Add Storage**.

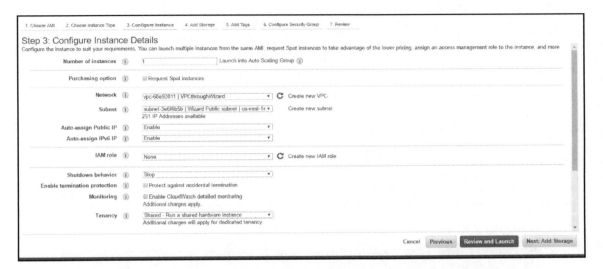

Choose network

6. Click on the **Advanced Details** and put the following lines in the text box. This is user data. This may vary with the OS of EC2. The script is executed when the instance is first created. Here is a script that can execute on Linux. It will install Apache, PHP, and MySQL in the server. It will also start the Apache server once the EC2 is running.

```
#!/bin/bash
yum update -y
yum install -y httpd24 php56 mysql55-server php56-mysqlnd
service httpd start
chkconfig httpd on
groupadd www
usermod -a -G www ec2-user
chown -R root:www /var/www
chmod 2775 /var/www
find /var/www -type d -exec chmod 2775 {} +
find /var/www -type f -exec chmod 0664 {} +
echo "<?php phpinfo(); ?>" > /var/www/html/phpinfo.php
```

7. Accept the default option and click **Next: Add Tags**.

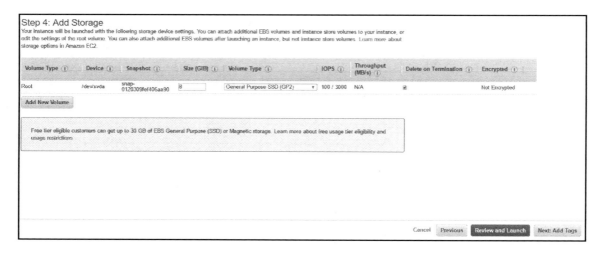

Add Storage

8. Click on **Add Tags**. In **Key**, put Name and in **Value**, put MyFirstEC2. Click on **Next: Configure Security Group**.

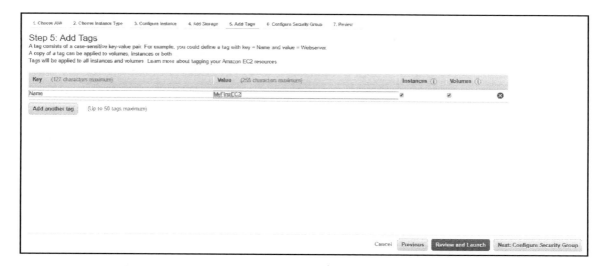

Add Tags

9. Provide a **Security group name** and **Description**. By default, SSH is open to all IP addresses. In **Source**, we have two CIDR ranges, **0.0.0.0/0** to allow all IPv4 addresses and **::/0** to allow all IPv6 addresses. Click on **Add Rule** and allow HTTP traffic to all source. We should not be opening our servers to all like this, however for simplicity, let's do this for now. Click on **Review and Launch**.

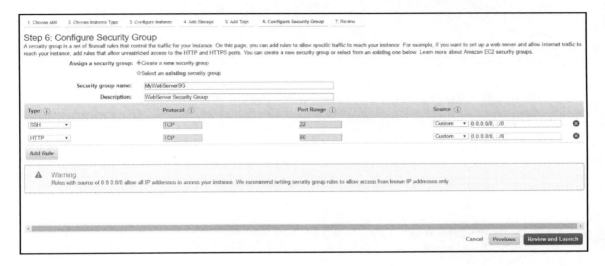

Configure Security Group

10. Review the details and click **Launch**.

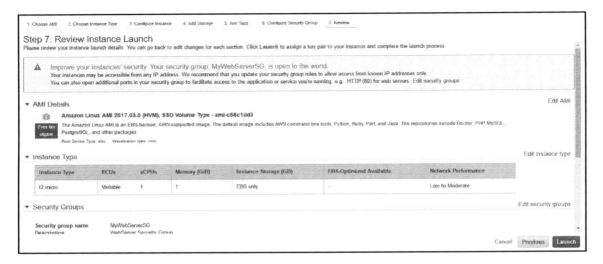

Review instance launch

11. We can optionally create a key pair. Key information is required if we want to log into EC2. **Download Key Pair** and store it in a safe place. Click on **Launch Instances**.

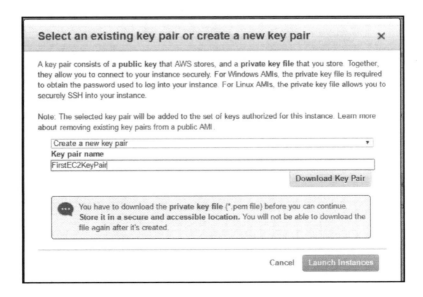

Create Key Pair

12. You can see a success message with the EC2 instance ID. Click on the ID. It will take us to the EC2 console. The instance will be in running condition in some time.

EC2 launch status

13. We can see both **Public DNS (IPv4)** and **IPv6 IPs**. We can create URL to access page running on EC2: `http:// DNS(IPv4)/phpinfo.php`. Replace the **DNS (IPv4)** in the URL with the one you see in the console. Open a browser and paste the URL.

EC2 instance detail

14. We can see the page of the server we created on the EC2 instance.

Sample web page on EC2

# How it works...

We have seen that the Network ACL with VPC and subnet allows all traffic. In the security group of the instance, we have opened HTTP protocol on port 80 for all incoming traffic. Internet Gateway is attached to the subnet in which we created the instance. During instance creation we have installed Apache, PHP and MySQL to host a website with page phpinfo.php. As we have enabled IPv4 and IPv6 in VPC, subnet and EC2, the EC2 instance has assigned those. So, after EC2 creation, we can access the website using the URL. The DNS name is resolved by AWS Route 53.

# Creating NAT on EC2 instance

In this recipe, you'll learn how to create a NAT instance on EC2 instances created in a public subnet. The private subnet does not have any Internet Gateway attached to it, so EC2 on private subnet cannot directly communicate with the outside world.

# Getting ready

We need an AWS account and user with proper permissions for creating a NAT instance on EC2. Create an EC2 in the same way as the previous recipe. The only difference is, you don't put any **Advanced Details** in the **Choose Network** page. In the security group page, create NATSG security group and attach the same with instance with the following rules. We are allowing all traffic for simplicity. However, you should only put the required CIDR ranges.

**NATSG: Rules**

| Inbound | | | |
|---|---|---|---|
| **Type** | **Protocol** | **Port range** | **Source** |
| **HTTP** | TCP | 80 | 0.0.0.0/0 and ::/0 |
| **HTTPS** | TCP | 443 | 0.0.0.0/0 and ::/0 |
| **SSL** | TCP | 22 | 0.0.0.0/0 and ::/0 |
| **Outbound** | | | |
| **Destination** | **Protocol** | **Port range** | **Comments** |
| **All traffic** | TCP | ALL | 0.0.0.0/0 and ::/0 |

You can use the same key pair created before for this instance as well. In the **Add tag** page, put **Nat Instance** in value for **Name** and **Key**. We also need to create an Elastic IP for attaching it to a NAT instance. This we shall show in the recipe.

# How to do it...

1.  I have created one more EC2 instance as visible in the **Instances** section of the EC2 console.

EC2 created for NAT

2.  Click on **Elastic IPs** in the left menu bar.

Elastic IP dashboard

3.  Click on **Allocate new address**.

Elastic IP creation page

4. Click on **Allocate**.

Elastic IP creation success message

5. Click on **Close**. The Elastic IP page will be visible. Choose **Elastic IP** and click on **Actions | Associate address**.

Elastic IP Action menu

6. Choose **Instance** in the **Resource type**. Select **Nat Instance** from the **Instance** drop-down menu. Click on **Associate**. A success message is shown.

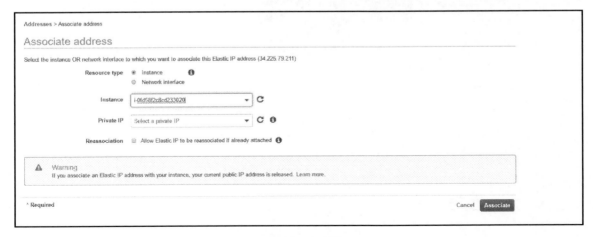

Elastic IP association with EC2 instance

7. Go to the **Instances** menu. You can see that the public DNS and IPv4 public IP has changed. You can see **Change Source/Dest. Check** is true for the instance.

EC2 instance with Elastic IP

8. Select **Actions** | **Networking** | **Change Source/Dest. Check**.

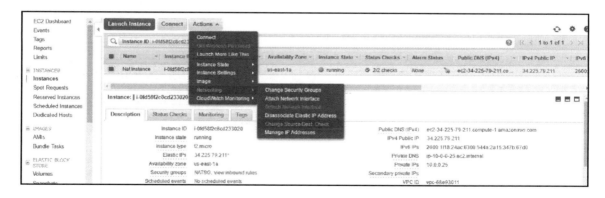

Changing Source/Dest Check for NAT instance

9. You can see that **Change Source/Dest. Check** is now false.

NAT instance details

10. We need to update the main Route Table attached to the VPC. Let's go back to the VPC dashboard and select our VPC.

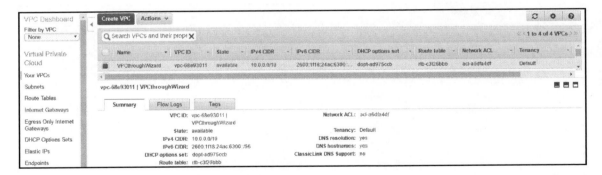

VPC dashboard

11. Click on the **Route Tables** starting with **rtb**.

Main Route Table

12. Select the Route Table and navigate to the **Routes** tab. Click on the **Edit** button. Add 0.0.0.0/0 in the destination and the NAT instance ID in **Target**. Click **Save**.

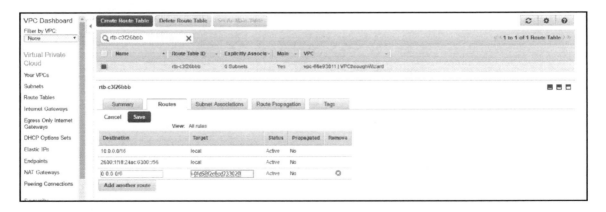

Attach NAT in main Route Table

# How it works...

By default, EC2 instance can either be a source or destination for network traffic request or response. However, NAT instances need to forward requests to the internet that were originated from a private subnet and return the response back to them. That's why we need to disable the source destination check for NAT instance.

# There's more...

NAT instance does not support IPv6. To support NAT for IPv6 we need to create an **Egress-Only Internet Gateway** from the VPC console and attach it to main Route Table.

# Working with network interfaces

**Elastic Network Interface (ENI)** in AWS is a network interface that can be attached to an EC2 instance. Based on its capacity, one EC2 instance can have number of ENIs attached to it. Each ENI comes with its own MAC and IP addresses. You can't move the ENI to another subnet after it is created. You can attach an ENI to an EC2 in the same AZ.

# Getting ready

We need an AWS account and user with proper permissions for creating an ENI.

# How to do it...

Here are the steps to follow:

1. Log in to the AWS account and browse to `https://console.aws.amazon.com/ec2/`. In the left navigation menu, choose **Network Interfaces**.

Network Interface Dashboard

2. Click on **Create Network Interface**.

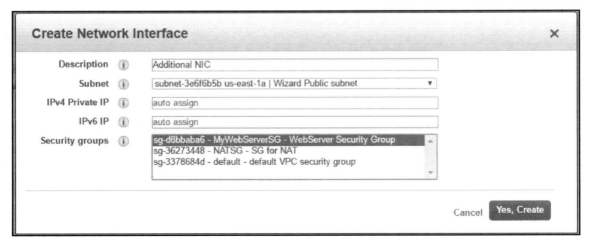

Network Interface Creation Details

3. In **Description**, provide the name. In **Subnet,** choose subnet where the NIC needs to be created. Leave **IPv4 Private IP** and **IPv6 IP**; they will be created as per CIDR range of subnet. Select **Security Group**. Otherwise, you can mention the IP address from the CIDR range. Click on **Yes, Create**.

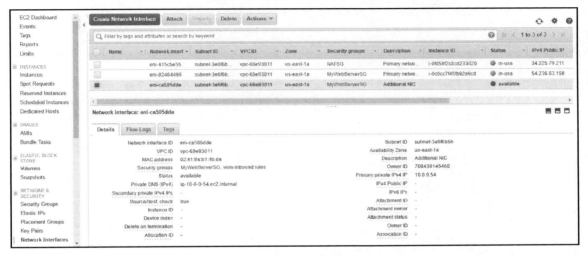

Network Interface Detail

4. You can see that only one network interface is created. However, its status is available as it is not attached to any instance. Click on the **Attach** button.

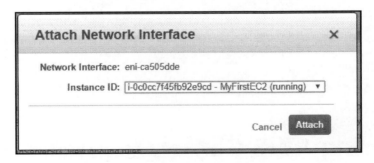

Network Interface Creation

5. Choose the EC2 **Instance ID** with which you want to attach it. Click **Attach**.

Network Interface attached

6. You can see that the interface is in use. You can **Detach** it and attach it to some other instance. From the **Action** menu you can manage the ENI. Click on **Instance ID**.

EC2 with two Network Interface

7. You can see two private IPs and two network interfaces **eth0** and **eth1**.

# Configuring AWS CLI

The AWS CLI is a collection of tools for managing AWS services from the command-line. We can create the script using CLI to automate AWS resource management. AWS CLI can be installed with an installer (Windows) or by using a `pip` or a package manager for Python.

# Getting ready

Keep the user access key details handy that we created in the earlier section.

# How to do it...

Here are the steps to follow:

- Installation for Windows:
    - Download the installer compatible with your system:
        - **Windows 64-bit**: https://s3.amazonaws.com/aws-cli/AWSCLI64.msi
        - **Windows 32-bit**: https://s3.amazonaws.com/aws-cli/AWSCLI32.msi
    - Run the installer and follow the instructions that appear
- Installation for Linux, macOS, or Unix:

    You should have a working version of Python 2.6.5+ or 3.5+ in your system. Otherwise, install python in your system first. Check your Python installation:

    ```
    $ python --version
    ```

    Follow the given steps to install AWS CLI using bundled installer:

    Download the AWS CLI bundled installer. For Linux flavor the command is as follows:

    ```
    $ cURL "https://s3.amazonaws.com/aws-cli/aws-cli-bundle.zip" -
    "awscli-bundle.zip"
    ```

    The package need to be unzipped. For Linux flavor the command is as following:

    ```
    $sudo ./awscli-bundle/install -i /usr/local/aws -b
    /usr/local/bin/aws
    ```

- Configuration:

  Type `aws configure` in command prompt or shell depending on your machine operating system. It will ask for the required details. Provide `AWS Access Key ID` and `AWS Secret Access Key` that were generated while creating an admin user. You can mention `us-east-1` as the default region or choose any other region from the list given in the screenshot following and `JSON` as `Default output format`. Don't worry if you don't understand region for now. We shall take a detailed look at in the following section.

```
C:\>aws configure
AWS Access Key ID :
AWS Secret Access Key :
Default region name :
Default output format:
```

Configure AWS CLI

You are all set for creating, modifying and managing networking components through API/CLI call in AWS depending on AWS privilege that your user have.

# 2
# Building Your Own Custom VPC

In this chapter, we'll cover the following recipes:

- Managing a VPC
- Managing public and private subnets
- Managing a Network ACL
- Managing a Security Group
- Managing an Internet Gateway
- Managing a NAT Gateway
- Managing a Route Table
- Managing EC2 instances

## Introduction

AWS provides a very user friendly interface for managing all of its services. This enables users to create services at the click of a button as and when required and delete them when they are not necessary. We shall go through recipes for creating the most used network components that we have to use, in case we host our application in AWS. Also, we shall learn how to create instances in the network that we built.

# Managing a VPC

AWS VPC is a virtual network in AWS cloud that is similar to the conventional network in a corporate data center. A VPC created in an account isolates all resources in it from any other VPC created by the same or other accounts.

## Getting ready

We need an AWS account and a user with proper permissions for creating a VPC.

## How to do it...

1. Log in to your AWS account. AWS provides a default VPC in each region where the account has been created, with all the components listed above in each **Availability Zone (AZ)** in that region. After logging in to the account, select **VPC** in **AWS services**:

Select VPC from AWS console

2. The VPC dashboard will appear. It is the place in the AWS console where you can manage all of the VPC and its related components. You need to select a different region from the top left menu option to see the VPCs and their related components for that region:

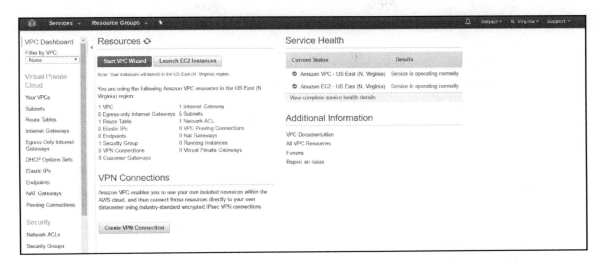

VPC dashboard

3. Click on **Your VPCs** in the VPC dashboard, the left menu option. We can see that the column **Default VPC** is **Yes**. This VPC has all components to host services in the cloud. This has been created to help new users create required resources in the VPC without understanding the complexity and relationship between different networking components in the VPC and without creating any of them:

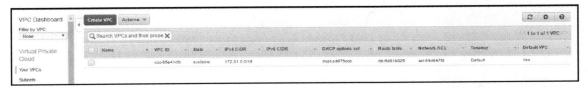

Default VPC

4. Click on **Create VPC**. Put the VPC name tag and CIDR range. If you need IPv6 support for components, select **Amazon provided IPv6 CIDR block**. Don't change the other options and click on **Yes, Create**:

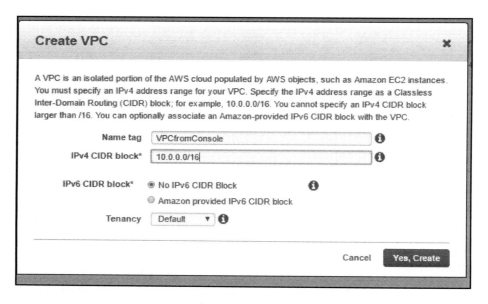

Creating VPC from console

5. A VPC is created with the given details. Please take note of the VPC ID. As we can see, a Route Table and Network ACL have also been created and associated with the VPC:

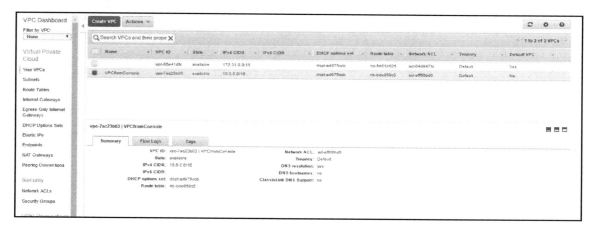

VPC dashboard with user created VPC from console

6. We can select a VPC and from the action menu, we can edit details or delete a VPC, as shown in the screenshot following:

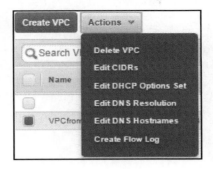

Modifying VPC details

# How it works...

The CIDR range decides the internal IPs of the EC2 instances created in the VPC. By default, the instances inside the same VPCs communicate with the internal IP. The number of instances that you can create is based on the CIDR range that you choose. If you want to communicate with an other network/VPC through a private network, the CIDR range of that network must be different.

# There's more...

By default, the same hardware hosts EC2 instances for multiple customers. If you need dedicated hardware for your instances, you should choose **Tenancy** as **Dedicated** during VPC creation. However, dedicated instances cost more.

# Managing public and private subnets

Subnets of AWS are similar to VLAN in DC with a specific range of IPs isolated from an other VLAN/subnet. Each AZ in a region can host multiple subnets, as per the requirement. A subnet is bound by one AZ limit and can't span across multiple AZs. There are two types of subnets; instances created in a public subnet are assigned a public IP and can be accessed from outside the VPC. There is another type of subnet that is called the private subnet. Public IP is not assigned to instance created inside this type of subnet. A default VPC has default subnets associated with it; all default subnets are public subnets.

# Getting ready

We need an AWS account and a user with proper permissions for creating a subnet.

# How to do it...

1. Click on **Subnets** in **VPC Dashboard**. You can see that one default subnet is created in each AZ available in that region associated with the default VPC:

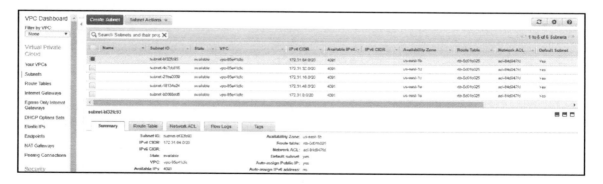

Default subnet

2. Click on **Create Subnet** link. Put the **Name tag,** select the **VPC**, CIDR range and **Availability Zone**. Click on **Yes, Create**:

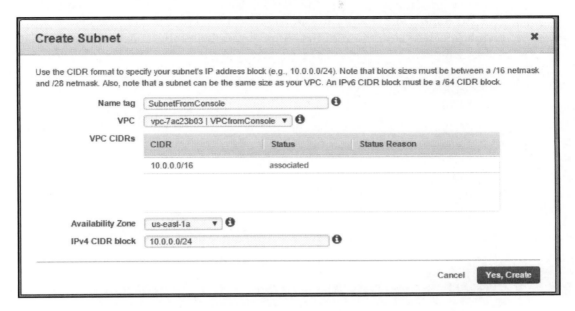

Create subnet from console

3. A subnet is created with the Route Table and the Network ACL. We can select a subnet and, from the **Subnet Actions** menu, delete a subnet or modify other settings:

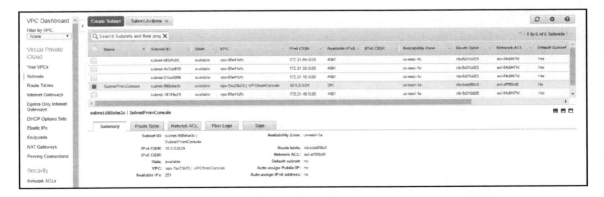

Dashboard with newly created subnet

4. Click on the **Route Table** tab. You can see two entries, one for local VPC communication and the other for external communication through the Internet Gateway (starting with `igw`). The Internet Gateway enables resources hosted in AWS to communicate with the outside world. As the subnet is capable of communication with the external world through an Internet Gateway, it is a public subnet:

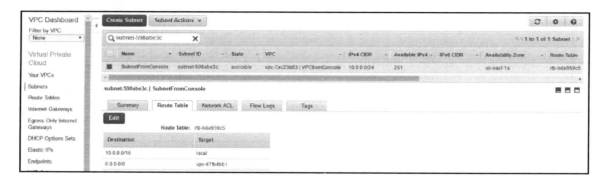

Route Table of subnet

5. Click on **Edit,** so we can change the Route Table. If we associate a subnet with the Route Table that does not have an IGW attached to it, the subnet will act as a private subnet because the external world cannot connect through it. In the later section, we'll see how to create a route table.
6. You can delete a subnet by choosing the **Delete** option from the **Subnet Actions** menu.

# There's more...

The CIDR range of a subnet determines the number of instances that can be created in a subnet and the internal IP range of the instances. The CIDR range of subnet should be a subset of the VPC CIDR range. Two subnets in a VPC can't have overlapping CIDR ranges.

# Managing a Network ACL

An AWS **Network Access Control List** (**NACL**) works as a firewall at the VPC level for controlling incoming and outgoing requests from one or more subnets associated with that VPC. It is used in conjunction with the **Security Group** (**SG**) in controlling traffic to the AWS. When we create a VPC, a default NACL is created that is open to every IP and port. The subnet is associated with the default NACL created during its creation. We can create a custom NACL and associate it with a subnet, thus replacing the default NACL.

## Getting ready

We need an AWS account and a user with proper permissions to create a security group. We also need to configure the AWS CLI in our local machine. We also need a VPC creation in the region where we are going to create the components. We have already created those in Chapter 1, *Getting Started with AWS Networking Components*.

## How to do it...

1. Log in to your AWS account and open the **VPC Dashboard**.

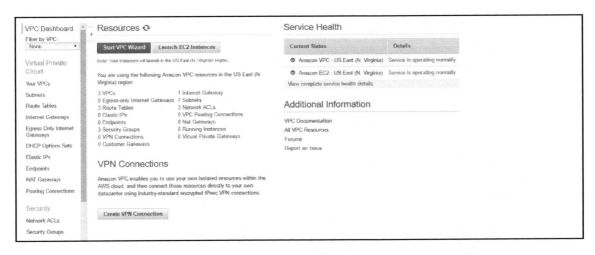

VPC Dashboard

2. Click on **Network ACLs** from the left menu bar under the **Security** menu. Default NACLs created with a default VPC and other VPCs that we created in `Chapter 1`, *Getting Started with AWS Networking Components*, appear on the screen. If you click on **Inbound Rules** and **Outbound Rules**, you will see that there is a rule number 100 which allows all traffic with all protocols from all ports. So effectively, the firewall is all open and traffic from any source, protocol, and port can connect to resources in this NACL. In the **Subnet Associations** tab, you can see that both subnets in the VPC are associated with NACL:

Default NACL

3. Click on **Create Network ACL** for creating a new NACL. Provide the **Name tag** and select the **VPC** for which you want to create an NACL. Click on **Yes, Create**:

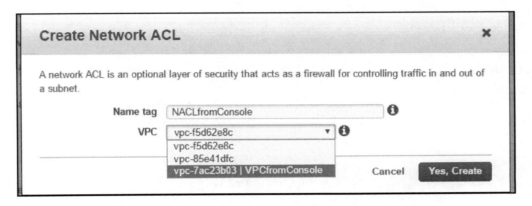

Network ACL creation from console

4. You can see that the **Default** column is **No** for the NACL that we just created. Click on **Inbound Rules** or **Outbound Rules**:

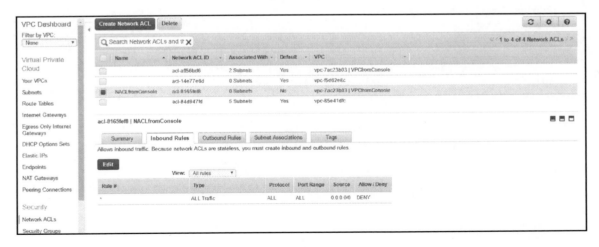

User created NACL

5. Click on the **Edit** button in the **Inbound Rules** tab. Click on **Add another rule**. You can add multiple rules. Here I am allowing all traffic for simplicity. Click on the **Save** button:

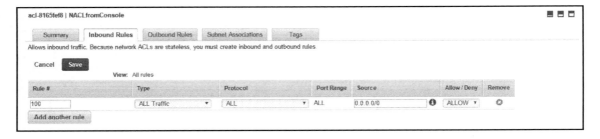

Add inbound rules to NACL

6. Click on the **Edit** button in the **Outbound Rules** tab. Click on **Add another rule**. You can add multiple rules. Here I am allowing all traffic for simplicity. Click on the **Save** button:

Add outbound rules to NACL

7. Click on **Subnet Associations**. Select the subnet that we created earlier. Click on the **Save** button:

NACL and subnet association

8. We can go and select the subnet menu and see that the NACL associated with the subnet has changed:

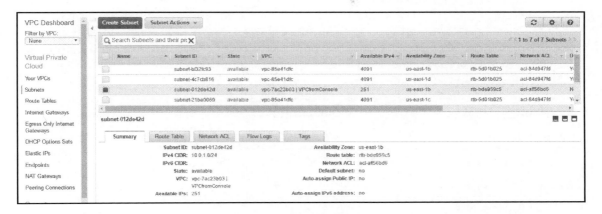

NACL and subnet association success

9. If a custom NACL is not associated with any subnet, it can be deleted by selecting the **Delete** button in the console. However, we can't delete the NACL that we created now as it is attached to a subnet. First we need to replace the subnet association, as given in step 7, and then can delete it if required.

# How it works...

We can define multiple inbound and outbound rules in an NACL. An NACL can be associated with one or multiple subnets in the VPC. An inbound rule allows or blocks incoming network requests from outside of the subnet to the resources hosted in the subnet. An outbound rule allows or blocks network requests from resources hosted within the subnet to outside of the subnet. Each rule has a number. The rules are evaluated from the rule with the lowest number first and then the rule with the next highest number. However, if a rule allows particular network traffic, other rules are not evaluated. So if a rule with the lowest number allows all traffic, more restrictive rule that would have blocked the traffic will not take effect. An NACL is stateless. This means that, if a network request is allowed by an inbound rule, the response can't go out if the outbound rule does not allow it, and vice versa. It may be preferable to add a DENY rule first where you want to allow a wide range of ports, but there are a few ports in that range which you would need to block.

# There's more...

When a request comes to a resource say, an HTTP request, a short-lived transport protocol port for **Internet Protocol (IP)** communications is allocated automatically from a predefined range by the IP stack software, and is called the ephemeral port. The response goes back via the ephemeral port. You need to know the ephemeral ports which differ depending on the OS; a few samples are shown in the table following. You need to allow ephemeral ports in an NACL for effective communication:

| Operating System | Ephemeral port |
|---|---|
| Amazon Linux | 32768-61000 |
| Windows Server 2003/Windows XP | 1025-5000 |
| Windows Server 2008 | 49152-65535 |
| AWS ELB/AWS NAT | 1024-65535 |

# Managing a Security Group

**Security Group (SG)** works as a virtual firewall that controls incoming traffic to protect resources hosted in AWS, such as EC2 and RDS, from unwanted access. The same SGs should be associated with services/resources having the same functionality and security requirements such as a cluster of web servers. SGs can span across different subnets in a VPC. SGs are stateful firewalls where you can define rules for a valid source, protocol, and port for incoming and outgoing traffic. Stateful meaning--if the connection from source to destination is allowed, the return path is also allowed. At least one SG needs to be attached to the resource at the time of resource creation. More than one SG can also be attached to a resource. The rules of an SG can be modified at any time and they will take effect immediately. An SG can be detached from the resource at any time.

# Getting ready

The prerequisites for this section are the same as recipe, *Managing a Network ACL*.

# How to do it...

1. Log in to your AWS account and open the **VPC Dashboard** as shown in the earlier recipe.
2. Click on **Security Group** in the left menu bar under the **Security** menu. The default SG created with the default VPC and other VPCs that we created in Chapter 1, *Getting Started with AWS Networking Components*, appears on the screen. If you click on **Inbound Rules** and **Outbound Rules**, you will see that all traffic, with all protocols from all ports, is allowed. So effectively, the firewall is all open and traffic from any source, protocol, and port can connect to the resources in this SG:

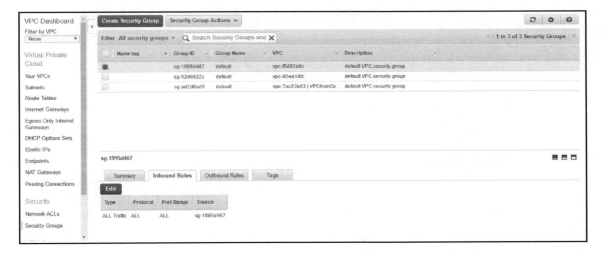

Default Security group

3. Click on **Create Security Group**. The following window will open. Put in the required details and the VPC with which you want to associate the SG. Click on **Yes, Create**:

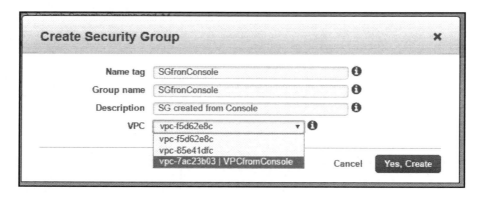

Security Group creation from console

4. You can now see the new SG. However, there is one important difference from the default SGs: there are no **Inbound Rules** defined. This means no traffic is allowed inside this SG:

Dashboard with created Security Group

5. Click on the **Edit** button under **Inbound Rules**. You can select the traffic type from the options. For now, put SSH. In the **Source**, you can mention any valid CIDR range, such as your corporate DC CIDR range. For now, put 0.0.0.0/0. You can also mention the security groups in the same VPC. You can add any additional inbound rules by clicking **Add another rule** and add HTTP, as shown. Click on the **Save** button:

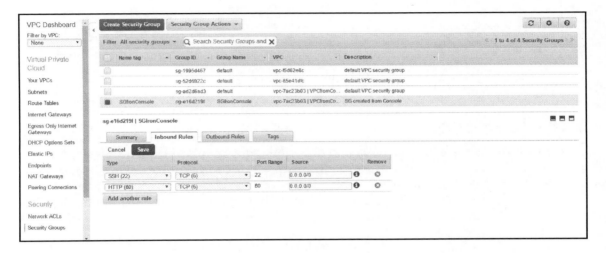

Configure Security Group inbound rule

6. You can see that the SG **Inbound Rules** has been saved successfully. Click on **Outbound Rules**. You can see that all outgoing traffic types to all ports and all destinations are allowed. For now, we are not modifying this. However, you can modify it if required:

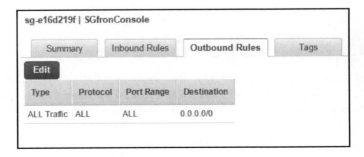

Security Group outbound rules

7. You can delete a particular SG by selecting **Delete Security Group** from the security group actions:

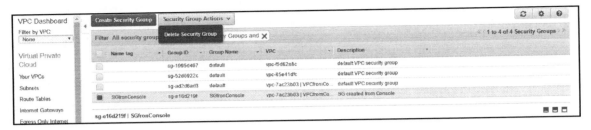

Delete Security Group

# How it works...

Security groups control the incoming and outgoing requests to and from resources hosted in the AWS. Inbound rules allow incoming network traffic from source CIDR ranges with the protocol and ports mentioned in a rule. If you want to allow requests only from resources hosted inside your VPC, put an SG associated with those resources in the source. Outbound rules allow outbound requests initiated from resources hosted in the AWS.

# There's more...

Apart from load balancers, the source for inbound rules should not be open to all IPs or ports for production scenarios. For other ports such as RDP/SSH, access should be allowed from the Jump Server/Bastion Host. All rules in an SG are evaluated before allowing any traffic.

# Managing an Internet Gateway

An Internet Gateway is an AWS component that enables communication between resources hosted in the VPC and the internet. It is a horizontally scalable and highly available component. It doesn't enforce any network bandwidth constraints. It is the channel through which services hosted inside the VPC are accessed by the outside world. It also enables resources hosted in the AWS to connect to the internet.

# Getting ready

The prerequisites for this section are the same as recipe, *Managing a Network ACL*.

# How to do it...

1. Log in to your AWS account and open the **VPC Dashboard** as shown in the earlier recipe.
2. Click on **Internet Gateways** in the left menu bar under the **Virtual Private Cloud** menu. You can see that the IG which was created with the default VPC in the region is visible:

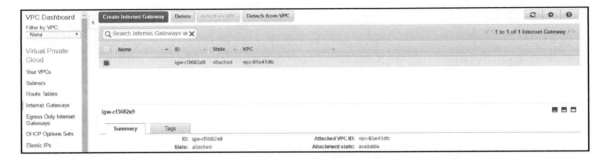

Internet Gateway dashboard

3. Click on **Create Internet Gateway**. The following window will open. Provide a **Name tag** and click on **Yes, Create**:

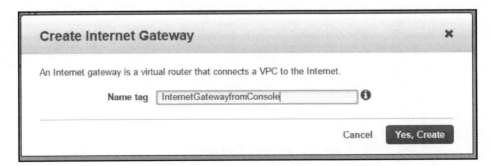

Internet Gateway creation from console

4. You can see the IG is created. However, it is in the detached state. This means that it is not attached to any VPC:

Dashboard with created Internet Gateway

5. Click on the **Attach to VPC** button. The following window will open. Select the **VPC** that we created and click on **Yes, Attach**:

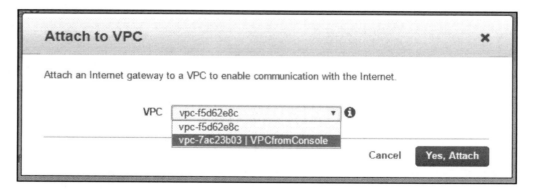

Attach Internet Gateway with VPC

6. Now you can see that the state of the IG has changed to **attached**:

| VPC Dashboard | Create Internet Gateway | Delete | Attach to VPC | Detach from VPC | | | | | |
|---|---|---|---|---|---|---|---|---|---|

Filter by VPC:
None

Virtual Private Cloud

Your VPCs

Subnets

Route Tables

Internet Gateways

Egress Only Internet Gateways

DHCP Options Sets

Elastic IPs

Endpoints

NAT Gateways

Q Search Internet Gateways ar ✕

1 to 2 of 2 Internet Gateways

| | Name | ▲ | ID | ▼ | State | ▼ | VPC | ▼ |
|---|---|---|---|---|---|---|---|---|
| ▪ | InternetGatewayfromConsole | | igw-d7fb4bb1 | | attached | | vpc-7ac23b03 | VPCfromConsole |
| | | | igw-cf3682a9 | | attached | | vpc-85e41dfc | |

igw-d7fb4bb1 | InternetGatewayfromConsole

Summary   Tags

ID: igw-d7fb4bb1 | InternetGatewayfromConsole

Attached VPC ID: vpc-7ac23b03 | VPCfromConsole

State: attached

Attachment state: available

Internet Gateway status

7. If you want, you can click on **Detach from VPC** and then **Delete** the IG that you created.

# How it works...

Resources inside the subnet only understand the private IP (internal) assigned to them from the CIDR range of that subnet. The default VPC has an IG attached to it and the subnet's route is associated with the IG. The IG works as a **Network Address Translation (NAT)** for instances that have public IP/Elastic IP attached to them. When outside instances send requests to the AWS resources with a public IP/Elastic IP, the IG translates the address and sends the request to the internal IP of the resource. Similarly, when resources inside a subnet send requests to services outside the VPC, the reply address is set by the IG as public/Elastic IP of that resource. Thus, if a subnet route has an IG attached to it, the resources hosted inside it are accessible from the internet. This type of subnet is called a **public subnet**. All default subnets are public subnets. If no IG is attached to the subnet route, the resources hosted inside it can't be accessed from the internet and is hence called a **private subnet**.

# There's more...

By default, all user created subnets are private subnets. If we want resources to be accessed from the internet directly, we need to create an IG and attach it to the VPC. The IG needs to be attached to the route table of the subnet that hosts the resources. If we attach an IG to the route of the subnet, it becomes a public subnet.

# Managing a NAT Gateway

By default, there is no way that resources hosted in a private subnet can access the internet. NAT is a way to achieve that. However, any resource outside the VPC can't access the resources in a private subnet. We can use a NAT instance or a NAT Gateway to achieve this. However NAT Gateway is a scalable, managed service that does not require any administration. In this section, we will see how to manage a NAT Gateway.

## Getting ready

We need to have an AWS account created with a user that has permissions to manage the NAT which we already have. We need to create an Elastic IP to be attached to with NAT, which is provided here. We shall learn details about Elastic IPs in the later sections.

## How to do it...

1. Log in to your AWS account and open the **VPC Dashboard** as shown in the earlier recipe.
2. Click on **Elastic IP** under the **Virtual Private Cloud** menu. There are no Elastic IPs as we have not created any till now:

Elastic IP console

3. Click on **Allocate New Address**. The following window will open. Click on **Allocate**:

Elastic IP creation from console

4. An Elastic IP will be provided:

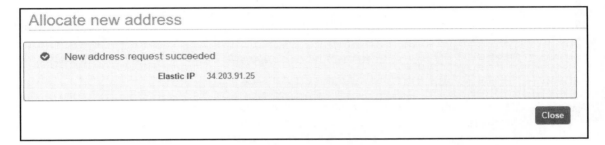

Console with Elastic IP created

5. Click on **NAT Gateways** under the **Virtual Private Cloud** menu:

NAT Gateway console

6. Click on **Create NAT Gateway**. The following window will open. Select the subnet where you want it to be hosted from the **Subnet** search menu and the Elastic IP that we created in step 4. Click on **Create a NAT Gateway**:

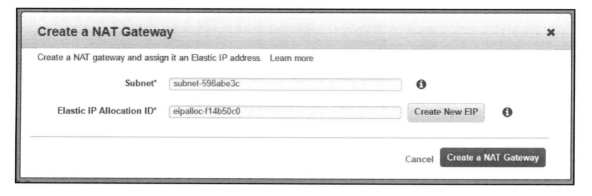

Console for NAT Gateway creation

7. You will get a confirmation message; you can see it on the dashboard. Initially, the **Status** will be **Pending**. The **Status** will change to **Available** after some time:

Console with created NAT Gateway

8. You can click on **Delete NAT Gateway** if it is not needed any more from the console. In that case, also remember to release the Elastic IP.

# How it works...

When resources in the private subnet need to connect to services out on the internet, they send the requests through NAT. NAT forwards the requests to the internet and replaces the return address of the Elastic IP address assigned to it instead with the internal IP of the resource. Similarly, when a response comes back, NAT translates the address to the internal IP of the resource and forwards the response.

# There's more...

A NAT instance is created in one subnet, meaning one AZ where the subnet is created. If you have resources in multiple AZs and in case the AZ that hosts the NAT Gateway is down, resources hosted in the other AZs lose the internet connection. So to have a highly available NAT infrastructure, you need to create a NAT Gateway which is a managed NAT service with a NAT instance created in multiple AZs to have fault tolerance.

# Managing a Route Table

A Route Table contains a set of rules that control how the network traffic flows within a VPC and outside of it. Each subnet must be associated with one Route Table. However, Route Tables may contain more than one subnet that needs the same route configuration.

# Getting ready

We need to have an AWS account created with a user that has permissions to manage Route Tables, which we already have. We have already created two subnets, one IG, and one NAT Gateway. By configuring these with the Route Table, we shall make one subnet a public subnet and the other one a private subnet.

# How to do it...

1. Log in to your AWS account and open the **VPC Dashboard** as shown in the earlier recipe.

2. Click on **Route Tables** under the **Virtual Private Cloud** menu. We can see the **Main** Route Table created and associated with the VPC that we created from the console. You can see that no subnet is associated with any route explicitly:

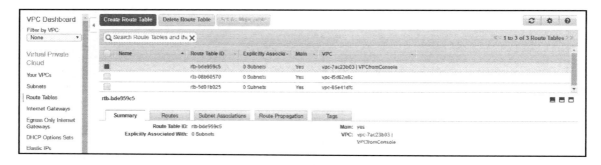

Route Table console

3. Click on **Routes**. You can see there is only one route with the **Target** as **local**. Click on **Edit**, and then click on **Add another route**. Add all destinations with 0 . 0 . 0 . 0 / 0 and target the Internet Gateway that we created earlier. Also, add the NAT Gateway in as another route. Click on the **Save** button:

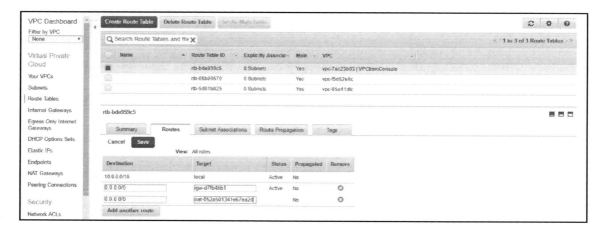

Configure main route table

4. Go to the **Subnet Associations** tab. You can see that no subnet is explicitly associated with this route:

Subnet association console for Route Table

5. Click on **Edit**. The following console will open. Select the subnet that we created from the console. Click on the **Save** button:

Edit subnet association for main route table

6. You can see that **Explicitly Association** has been modified from 0 to 1:

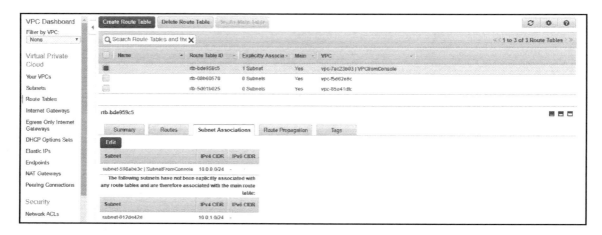

Route Table subnet association

7. Let's add another route for creating a private subnet. Click on **Create Route Table**. The following window will open. Put the **Name tag** and select the **VPC** that we created from the console earlier. Click on **Yes, Create**:

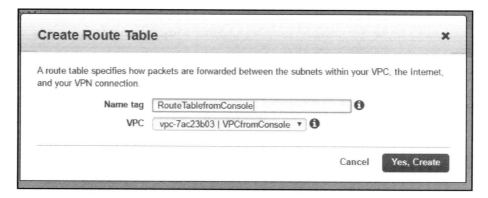

Console for Route Table creation

8. We can see the newly created Route Table in the console. However, the **Main** column is **No** for this case:

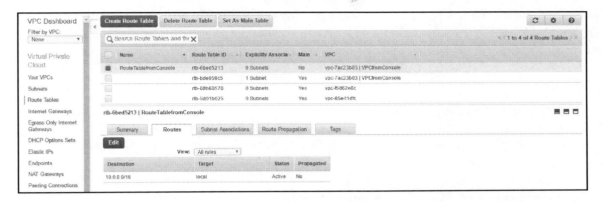

Console with custom route table

9. Go to **Subnet Associations**. Click on the **Edit** button. Choose the other subnet that we created. Click on the **Save** button:

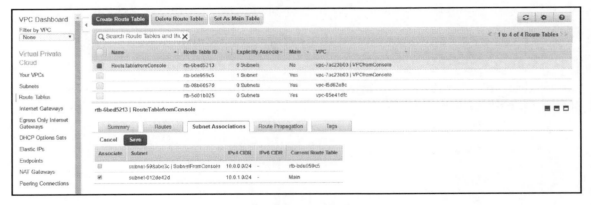

Subnet association for custom route table

10. After removing the subnet association with a particular route table, you can delete it by clicking the **Delete Route Table** button.

# How it works...

Now we have turned one subnet into a public subnet that is associated with the route table having Internet Gateway and NAT Gateway. The other subnets that are associated with the route table with a local route become private subnets.

# There's more...

A VPC comes with a main router when created. If any subnet in the VPC is not associated with any route table, it is automatically associated with the main table. You can make any Route Table the main table by clicking the **Set As Main Table** button from the console.

# Managing EC2 instances

EC2 is an infrastructure in the AWS Cloud with certain compute, memory, and network resources. Though EC2 is not a networking component, we shall try to create a couple of them to check whether the network components that we have created work with EC2. We shall also understand how networking components integrate with resources in AWS.

# Getting ready

We need to have an AWS account created with a user that has permission to manage EC2 instances, which we already have.

# How to do it...

1. Log in to your AWS account and open the **EC2 Dashboard**:

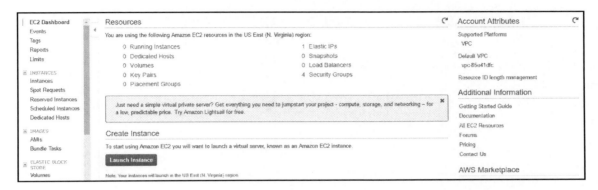

EC2 Dashboard

2. Click on the **Launch Instance**. The following window will open. You can choose any prebuilt virtual image called **Amazon Machine Images (AMIs)** that you like. However, for now **Select** the first one:

Choose AMI for EC2

3. The following window will open. Select the instance type that you would like to choose. For now, select the one that is already selected. It is free tier eligible:

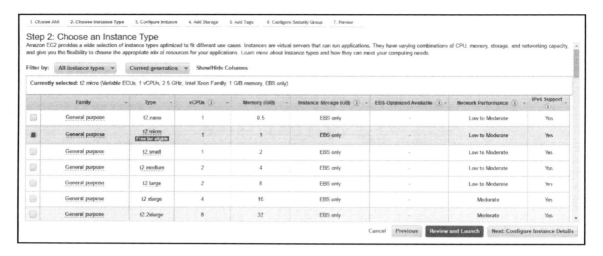

EC2 - Choose instance type

4. Click **Next: Configure Instance Details**. The following window will open. In the **Number of instances**, put 1. You can create more by putting a higher number. In **Network**, choose the VPC that we created earlier. In **Subnet**, choose the public subnet that we created earlier. In **Auto-assign Public IP**, choose Enable. Leave other options as they are. Click on **Next: Add Storage**:

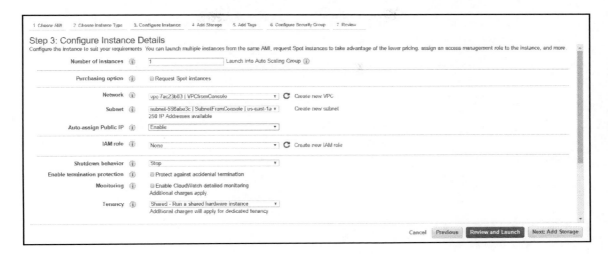

Configure EC2 Network detail

5.  Leave the details as they are and click on **Next: Add Tags**:

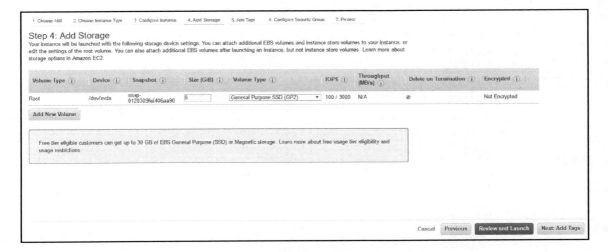

Choose EC2 Storage

6. Add a tag for identifying the EC2 instance in the EC2 dashboard. Click on **Next: Configure Security Group**:

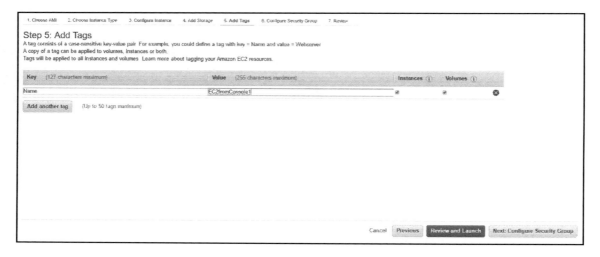

Add EC2 tag

7. Select the **Select an existing security group** option. It will show the SG that we created earlier. Choose it. Click on **Review and Launch**:

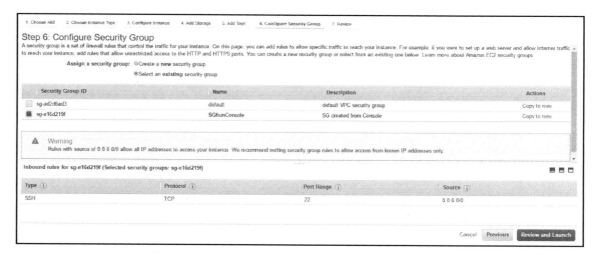

Choose EC2 SG

8. Review the details and click **Launch**:

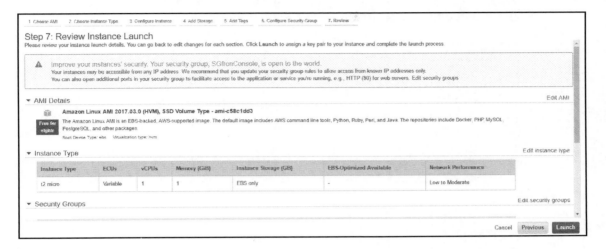

Launch EC2

9. The following window will open. Select **Create the new key pair** and **Key pair name**. Download the key and store it. We shall use it in a while. Click on the **Launch Instances** button. You will get a success message:

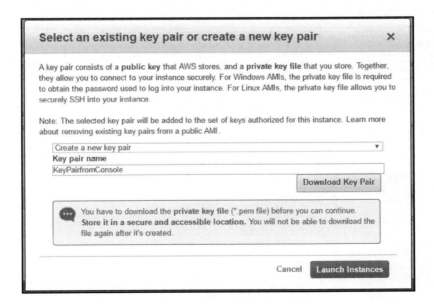

EC2 Key Pair creation

10. Go to the EC2 dashboard. Select **Instances** from the **Instances** menu. Choose the instance that we just created. You will see the details about the instance. You can also see that the public IP has been assigned to it:

EC2 instance details

11. Click on the **Connect** button. You can see the instructions to connect to the instance using an SSH client. If you would have chosen Windows AMI, it would show the connection steps using RDP. You should be able to connect to the instance using the public IP of the instance. For details, please refer to the AWS Documentation (http://docs.aws.amazon.com/AWSEC2/latest/UserGuide/putty.html):

Connecting to EC2 instance

12. You can terminate or stop an instance from the **Instance State** of the **Action** menu when needed.

# How it works...

This EC2 instance is created in a public subnet that has an IGW attached to it. The NACL is open for all connections. Security groups is open to all inbound connections over port 22, so we could add SSH to the instance.

# There's more...

The public IP associated with the instance is transient. If we stop and start the instance, the IP will change. We can attach the Elastic IP to the instance in the same way we attached the Elastic IP to the NAT instance in `Chapter 1`, *Getting Started with AWS Networking Components*. In that case, the IP will not be changed if the instance is stopped and started.

If we had created an instance in a private subnet, it could not have been connected as there is no inbound route available from the internet. However, we can connect to it from the instance in the public instance. For that, we need to add an SG of the public subnet instance to the inbound rules of an SG of the private instance. Once we log into the private subnet instance, we can connect to the internet as we have configured the NAT Gateway.

# 3
# VPC Advanced Components

In this chapter, we'll cover the following recipes:

- Assigning multiple IPs to an instance and ENI
- Accessing an instance within the network
- Accessing an instance from outside AWS
- Creating an application ELB
- Creating a launch configuration
- Creating an Auto Scaling group
- Creating VPC peering
- Accepting VPC peering
- Configuring VPN connections to your Amazon VPC

## Introduction

In this chapter, we shall dive further to learn to create components for load balancing of an application. Load balancing is required to route the request to different servers hosting the applications. This helps to host applications with the exact capacity that the application needs at a certain point of time.

Security is a major concern that cuts across every application type. We shall learn how to build components for establishing communication between multiple VPCs and between a data center and VPC. This will enable applications and services to securely connect to each other.

# Assigning multiple IPs to an instance and ENI

The **Elastic Network Interface (ENI)** is a virtual interface. Any instance when created comes with its default NI attached to it (eth0). Additional ENIs can be created and attached to an instance or can be detached from it. The number of ENIs that can be attached to an EC2 instance depends on its type. An ENI may have the following properties:

- One primary and multiple secondary IPv4 addresses and optionally, one public or Elastic (fixed) IPv4 IP
- One or more IPv6 addresses if supported by the instance type and network
- One MAC address
- Additional properties such as SG, source destination check, and so on.

This recipe is similar to creating a NAT instance that we learnt in Chapter 1, *Getting Started with AWS Networking Components*. In that case, we attached an Elastic IP to one instance. Here, we shall learn how to create an ENI and attach it to an EC2 instance. For an ENI to be attached to an EC2, it must be done in same subnet and VPC.

## Getting ready

Log in to the console with the appropriate permission.

## How to do it...

The stepsfor assigning multiple IPs to an instance are as follows:

1. Go to the AWS EC2 console by typing the URL in your favorite browser: https:/ /console.aws.amazon.com/ec2/. Choose **Network Interfaces** in the left navigation menu under **Network & Security**. In the dashboard, you can see the ENI that has already been created while creating the EC2 instance or the Elastic IP. Click on **Create Network Interface**:

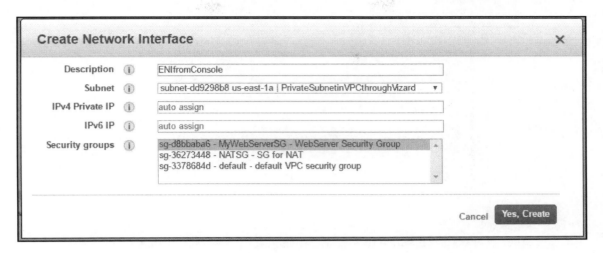

Crete network interface

2. Provide the **Description** and select the **Subnet** to which it should be associated with. Choose the **IPv4 Private IP** and **IPv6 IP** that is allowed under the CIDR of the subnet. You can leave it and AWS will choose the IPs for you. Select the **Security groups** that it should be associated with. SGs created in the VPC will be populated in the **Security groups** section. Click **Yes, Create**. We can change the Security Group associated with the ENI later.

3. You can now see the **Network Interface** that was just created in the dashboard. You can see the status is **available**:

Create network interface

4. Click on the **Attach** button:

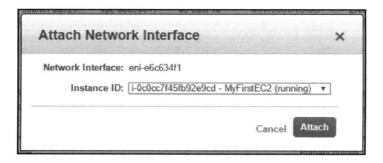

Attach network interface

5. Select the EC2 instance that you want to attach the ENI with. Click on the **Attach** button:

Network interface attached

6. You can see that the status has changed to **in-use**. The **Instance ID** of the EC2 instance is visible in the **Details** section. If you want, you can detach the network interface and attach it with another instance in the same subnet.

# There's more...

Now the EC2 instance has two ENIs attached to it. So, the instance can be connected using any IP associated with either of the ENIs based on the SG rules attached to the ENI.

A network interface can be attached to an instance in the running state, stopped state, or while the instance is being created. An Elastic IP is a special network interface and it can be attached to any instance in the public subnet in any VPC of your account. In Chapter 1, *Getting Started with AWS Networking Components*, we created one EIP while creating a NAT instance.

# Accessing an instance within the network

In the earlier chapters, we created an instance in the public subnet and connected to it from our system. In this section, we shall create an instance in the private subnet of the same VPC and connect it from the instance that we created earlier. We shall create a private subnet in the VPC that we created in Chapter 1, *Getting Started with AWS Networking Components*, and create an instance to it.

# Getting ready

Log in to the account with the proper permissions and a VPC, subnet, and EC2 instance in the public subnet already created.

# How to do it...

The steps for accessing an instance within the network are as follows:

1. Log in to the AWS console EC2 dashboard by browsing to the URL `https://console.aws.amazon.com/vpc/`. Choose **Subnet** from the left side menu. Click on **Create Subnet**. Provide the required details. Click on **Yes, Create**:

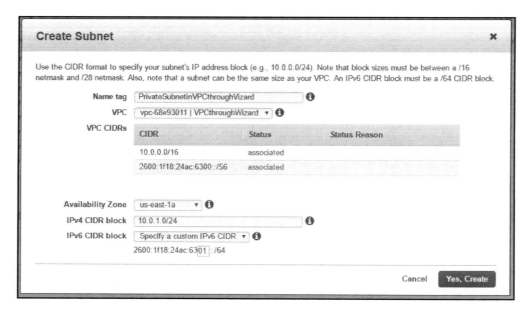

Create private subnet

2. You can create an EC2 instance by following the similar steps provided in `Chapter 2`, *Building Your Own Custom VPC*. We need to create it in the subnet that we just created and assign an SG to allow only instances in the public subnet to connect to it. Let's create an instance from the existing one. Browse to **Instances** in the **EC2 Dashboard**. Select one EC2 instance that you want to create a new EC2 instance from. Go to **Actions** | **Launch More Like This**:

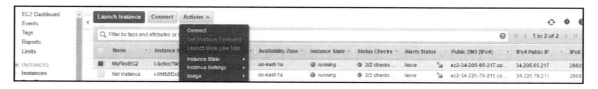

Create similar EC2 instances

3. The EC2 creation review page will appear as follows:

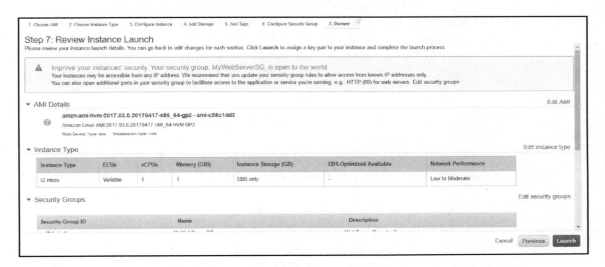

EC2 creation review page

4. Click on **Edit instance type**. Change the **Subnet** to the newly created one. Click on **Review and Launch**:

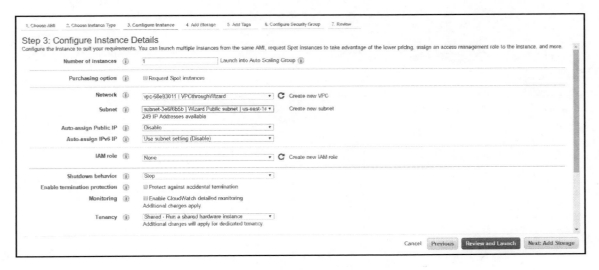

Modify configure instance details

5. You will come back to the preview page. Click on **Edit security groups**. Choose **Create a new security group**. Put the **Security group name** and **Description** for all the rules for the Security Group. Here we'll open port 22 for instances created in the Security Group associated to the instance created in the public subnet. Copy the SG associated with that instance and paste it in **Source**:

Modify Security Group

6. Click **Review and Launch** and then click on **Edit Tag**. Put the tag as per your needs:

Add EC2 tag

7. Click **Review and Launch**. Click on **Launch**. You can create a new key or use an existing key. I'll be using the existing one. Click on **Launch Instances**:

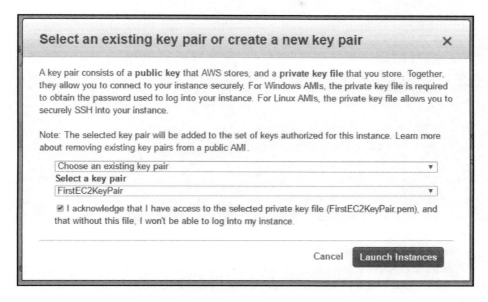

Launch EC2 instance

8. You will see a success page as shown:

EC2 Create success message

9. Click on the instance ID. Wait for some time till it comes to the running state with status checks in green. First, log in to the public subnet EC2 instance `MyFirstEC2` in the same way we did in `Chapter 1`, *Getting Started with AWS Networking Components*:

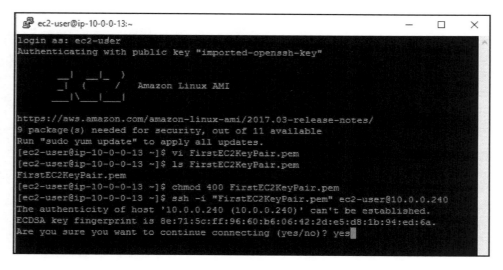

Connect to EC2 instance in public subnet

10. Create a file using your favorite editor. Paste the contents of the EC2 key you downloaded earlier and save it. Verify that the file has been created, and modify its permission to 400 (`chmod 400 FirstEC2KeyPair.pem`), and connect to it (`ssh -i <KeyName> ec2-user@<Private IP of instance>`). Type `yes` for continuing the connection:

Connect to EC2 instance in private subnet

11. You will be logged in to the instance in the private subnet. You can see that the IP of EC2 console has changed to one of private subnet (10.0.0.240) from one in public subnet (10.0.0.13).

Connection to private subnet EC2 instance successful

# How it works...

EC2 instances in a VPC can connect to each other via the local route in the Route Table provided the Security Group allows inbound connections. For SG (say SGPrivate) of the instance in private subnet, we added SG of instance in public subnet(say SGPublic). This ensures that no other instance can connect to the new instance in the private subnet apart from EC2 instances associated with SGPublic. Now we have created a bastion server or jump server, which is our EC2 instance in the public subnet. To connect to the instance in the private subnet instances, someone has to go through it. Generally, the Security Group of a **bastion** server is configured to accept connections from a list of known IP addresses where administrators operate from.

# Accessing an instance from outside AWS

In the last recipe, we connected to an instance in the private subnet through a bastion server through the internet. In this recipe, we'll see how to connect to the Windows Server and connect it through the Microsoft **Remote Desktop Protocol** (RDP). You need to have a Windows OS in your machine to complete this recipe.

# Getting ready

Log in to the console with the appropriate permissions.

# How to do it...

The steps for accessing an instance from outside AWS are as follows:

1. Browse to the EC2 console. Click on **Launch Instance**. Select **Microsoft Windows Server 2016 Base** AMI:

Choose Windows AMI

2. Select t2.micro on the **Choose Instance Type** page. Click on **Next: Configure Instance Details**. Select a VPC in **Network** and a public subnet in **Subnet** with **Auto-assign Public IP** enabled. Click **Next: Add Storage**. Let the default option be there and click **Next: Add Tags**. Let the default option be there and click **Next: Configure Security Group**:

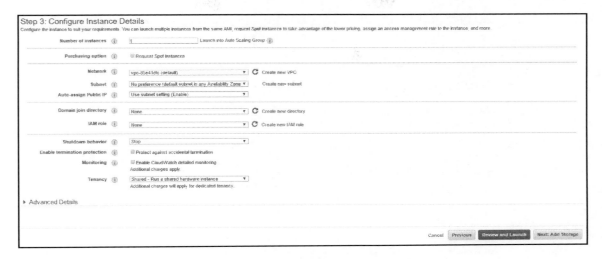

Choose configuration details

3. You can see that the port **RDP** is open for all IP addresses. You may modify the IP range to suit your needs:

Security group for Windows instance

4. Click **Review and Launch** and then click on **Launch**. Select **Choose an existing key pair** and click on **Launch Instance**. You can see the instance in the **EC2 Dashboard** with the public IP assigned to it:

Windows instance on EC2 console

5.  Choose EC2 and click on **Connect**. Click on **Download Remote Desktop File** and save it.

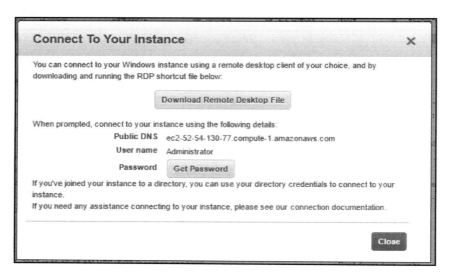

Windows instance connection guideline

6.  Click on **Get Password,** the following window will open. Select the **Key Pair Path**. Click on **Decrypt Password**. The password will be shown. Copy the password and save it.

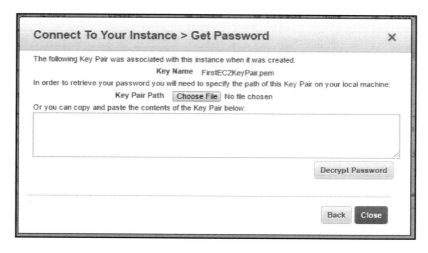

Windows instance password generation

7. Click on the RDP shortcut downloaded earlier. Put in the user ID and password. You will now be able to connect to the instance.

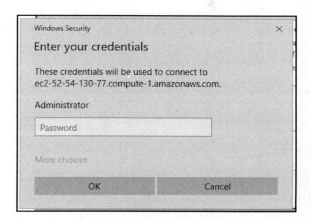

Windows Instance Connection

# Creating an application ELB

AWS provides an **Elastic Load Balancer (ELB)** as a service. AWS has two kinds of ELB:

- Classic ELB
- Application Load Balancer

A Classic ELB can forward requests to one set of EC2 instances and an Application Load Balancer can forward requests to applications based on the application content/path/host. Classic load balancer can handle load for both layer 4 and layer 7. Application load balancer can handle load for only layer 7 protocol.

# Getting ready

Login to the console with appropriate permissions.

# How to do it...

The steps are as follows:

1.  Browse to AWS EC2 console by typing the URL: `https://console.aws.amazon.com/ec2`. Click on **Load Balancers** under the **LOAD BALANCING** option on the left menu. Click on **Create Load Balancer**:

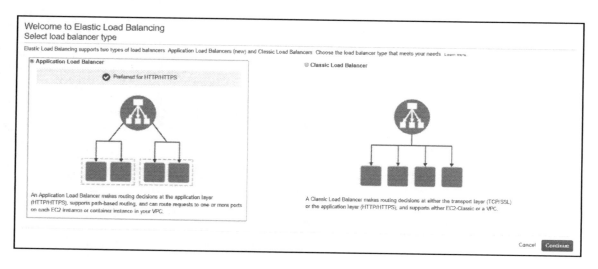

Select Load Balancer Type

2.  Let's choose the **Application Load Balancer** and click **Continue**. Provide the load balancer **Name, Scheme,** whether it is internet facing or internal facing and the **IP address type** for only IPv4 support of dual stack support. If you choose dual stack, your VPC and subnets should have support for IPv4 and IPv6 ports. Provide **Listeners** on which protocol (HTTP/S) and port you want the requests to come to. Scroll down to select the **VPC** where you want to create the load balancer and select at least two Availability Zones where the load balancer instances will be created. To have an internet facing load balancer, subnets need to have an IGW attached to them. You can add tags as well. Click **Next: Configure Security Settings**:

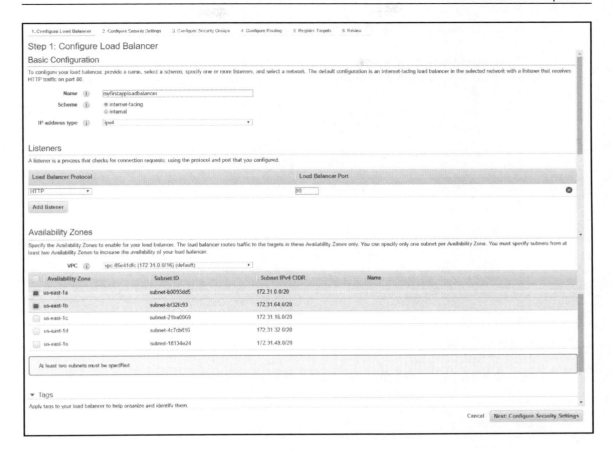

Select security setting

3. If you choose the HTTPS listener, you need to provide a security certificate. As I have chosen HTTP, no configuration is required in this step. Click on **Next: Configure Security Group**. Choose **Create a new security group**. Provide the **Security group name** and **Description**. Provide rules and as we chose HTTP protocol and port 80 in the previous step, keep the same here. In the source, you can put the source IP range that you want the request coming from. I am allowing all URLs by providing the CIDR range to be open to all:

Configure Security Group

4. Click on **Next: Configure routing**. Provide the name of the target group. It is a logical group of all the servers that the load balancer sends traffic to. Provide the **Protocol** and **Port** that the services on the server are running on. Provide the **Health Checks** details using which load balancer sends requests at regular intervals to verify whether the server is healthy or not:

Configure load balancer routing

5. It will provide a list of EC2 instances already running. As we don't have any instance in the VPC, the list is empty. You can choose instances if there are any. However, you need to remember that merely adding those instances will not work. The service should be up and should provide a healthy response to the health check settings which you did earlier and Security Group of server should be modified to allow incoming requests from the ELB. Click on **Next: Review**.

6. Review the details and click **Create**. Success message will be displayed. Click on **Close**. You'll be able to see the application load balancer created with all details. You can see the **DNS name** of the load balancer which can be used to access the service hosted by the target group servers:

Load balancer details

# How it works...

The load balancer sends requests using the **Protocol** and **Path** that you provide in the **Health checks**. It initiates a request at a given interval to all server associated with it. If some server does not respond back in predefined interval for few consecutive requests, the server is marked as **OutOfService**. Load balancer does not send user requests to it. However load balancer keeps on sending the health check request. If server responds back to few consecutive health check requests, it is marked as **InService**. Load balancer send user requests to it again. **Advanced health check settings** provide better control on frequency of these requests and threshold to decide whether the server is healthy or not. Click on **Next: Register Targets**.

# There's more...

You can check the health of the ELB by looking at the monitoring tab. Different useful statistics including the number of requests and number of errors are provided. In Listener, you get an option to add another application group to forward the request to.

# Creating a launch configuration

A launch configuration is a way to create a template for creating EC2 instances that have the same predefined configuration. EC2 instances can be created when more instances are required for load balancing from this configuration.

# Getting ready

Log in to the console with the appropriate permissions.

# How to do it...

The steps for creating a launch configuration are as follows:

1. Browse to AWS EC2 console by typing the URL: `https://console.aws.amazon.com/ec2`. Browse to **Launch Configurations** under **AUTO SCALING** in the left menu bar. You'll see the following dashboard if there are no Auto Scaling Groups or launch configurations already created:

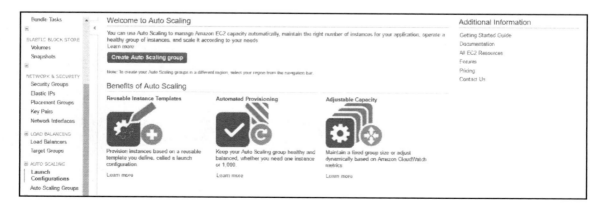

Create launch configuration

2. Click on **Create Auto Scaling group**:

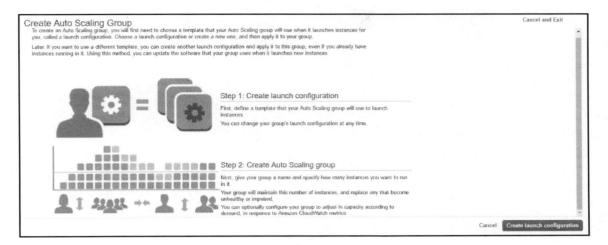

Create Auto Scaling group page

3. This page has an introduction and tells you that you need to create a launch configuration before creating an Auto Scaling group. Click on **Create launch configuration**. You will be taken through the same steps that you did while creating an EC2 instance. Select your favourite AMI by clicking on **Select** as shown following:

Choose AMI for launch configuration

4. Choose the instance type that you need to create:

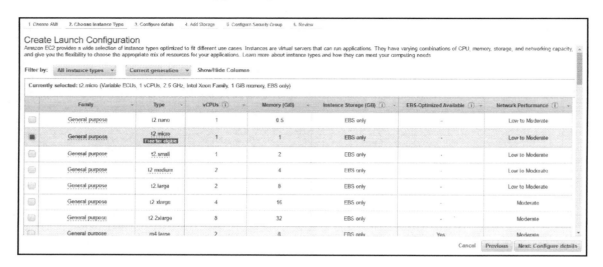

Choose instance type for launch configuration

5. Click **Next: Configure details**. Provide the **Name**. Click on the **Advanced Details** and put the following lines in the textbox. It will install Apache, PHP, and MySQL in the server. It will also start the Apache server once the EC2 is running:

```
#!/bin/bash
yum update -y
yum install -y httpd24 php56 mysql55-server php56-mysqlnd
service httpd start
chkconfig httpd on
groupadd www
usermod -a -G www ec2-user
chown -R root:www /var/www
chmod 2775 /var/www
find /var/www -type d -exec chmod 2775 {} +
find /var/www -type f -exec chmod 0664 {} +
echo "<?php phpinfo(); ?>" > /var/www/html/phpinfo.php
```

In the **IP Address Type**, choose the option **Do not assign a public IP address to any instances**, as we want to access the instances only through the load balancer:

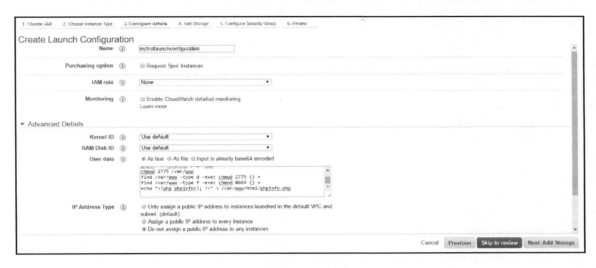

Choose configure details for launch configuration

6. Click on **Next: Add Storage**. You can modify it if you want large volumes to be attached to the EC2 instance. Leave the default options for now. Click on **Next: Configure Security Group**. Provide the **Security group name** and **Description**. Change the request protocol **Type** to HTTP and the **Port Range** to 80, as we did that in the load balancer configuration. In **Source**, choose **Custom IP** and provide the load balancer security group that we created earlier:

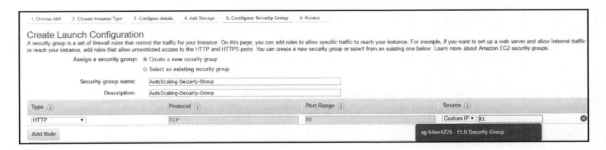

Choose add storage for launch configuration

7. Click on **Review**. You can review and modify configurations of the previous steps. Click on **Create launch configuration**:

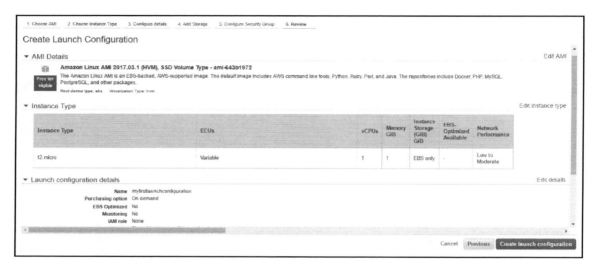

Review for launch configuration

8. Choose a key if you want to connect to the EC2 instance. But remember, you also need to add a security group of your bastion server in the same VPC in the **Configure Security Group** step; because, through the bastion server, you can connect to instances in the Auto Scaling group as these EC2 instances don't have a public IP. Check the acknowledgement and click on **Create launch configuration**:

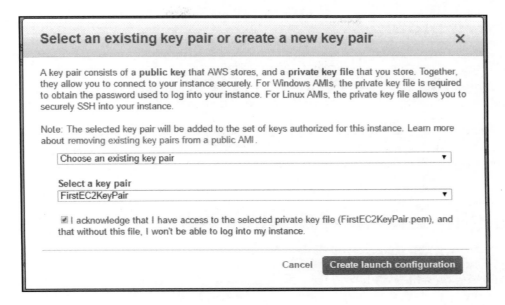

Select EC2 key for launch configuration

9. Click on the **Launch Configuration** menu again. You will see the dashboard with the launch configuration which we just created:

Figure 3 – 36 Launch configuration created

# There's more...

Generally, we create an EC2 instance and configure it with the required software and create a virtual image (AMI) from that EC2 from the EC2 **Actions** | **Image** | **Create Image** menu. Other compatible virtual machine images can also be imported to AWS for reuse. If we have created any, this will be visible under the **My AMIs** menu.

So instead of using boot strap scripts in step 5, we can use custom AMI to create ec2 instances. As the software already installed in EC2, it takes lesser time to start server. It is more useful when we have to install larger software that takes significant time.

# Creating an Auto Scaling group

An Auto Scaling group is a group of instances that host the same application. These instances are treated as a logical group for managing and scaling instances. You can define a criteria based on which of the number of instances serving the application can be changed to support the load on the application.

## Getting ready

Log in to the console with the appropriate permissions.

## How to do it...

The steps for creating an auto scaling group are as follows:

1. Browse to the AWS EC2 console by typing the URL: `https://console.aws.amazon.com/ec2`. Browse to **Auto Scaling Groups** under **AUTO SCALING** in left menu bar. You'll see the following dashboard if there are no Auto Scaling groups or launch configurations already created:

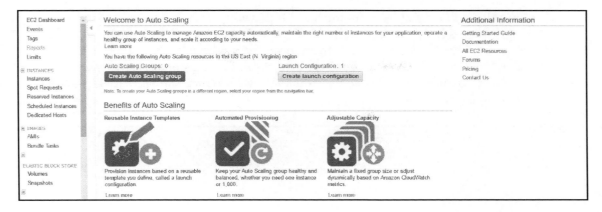

Create Auto Scaling Group

2. Click on **Create Auto Scaling group**. The following screen will appear. You can create a new launch configuration or select the existing one and click on **Next Step**:

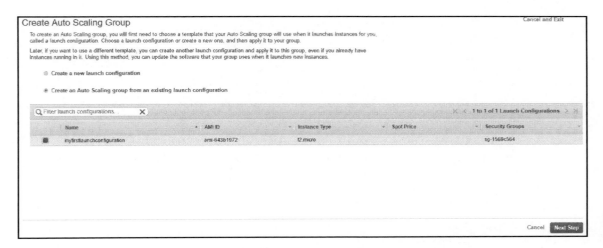

Create Auto Scaling group with launch configuration

3. Provide a name in **Group name** and **Group size** to create the minimum number of instances in the group. Select VPC in the **Network** option and one or more subnets to provide the AWS information about where these instances will be created. Leave the **Advanced Details** as they are. Click **Next: Configure scaling policies**. You should choose the same VPC with which the Security Group of the launch configuration is associated:

Create Auto Scaling Group Details

4. You can keep the group at its initial size. Otherwise define policies when you need to increase number of instances in group and reduce number of instances in the group. You provide the minimum and maximum instances in the group:

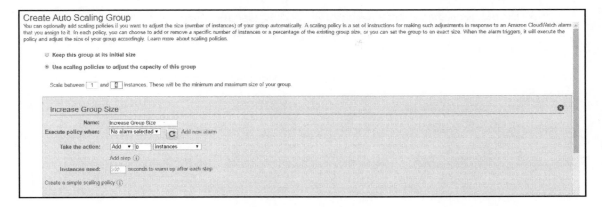

Create Auto Scaling group capacity

5. You need to click on the **Add new alarm** link to increase and decrease the group size sections. You can see we are defining policies to add new instances in the group; you can select from different parameters and conditions. You can optionally define the notification group to send an email when this event occurs. Here I have defined a policy to add an instance if the average CPU utilization of the instances in the group is more than or equal to 70% for at least 5 minutes. Click on **Create Alarm**:

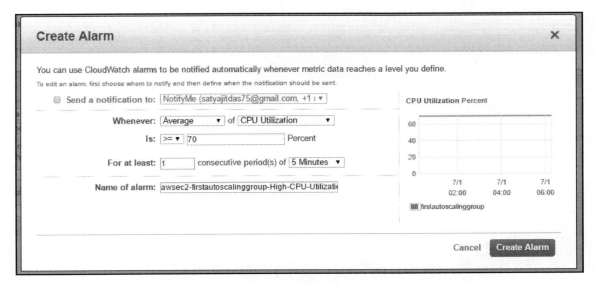

Alarm for increase group size

6. Similarly, we can define the policy to decrease the number of instances in the group if the average CPU utilization of the instances in the group is less than or equal to 30% for at least 5 minutes:

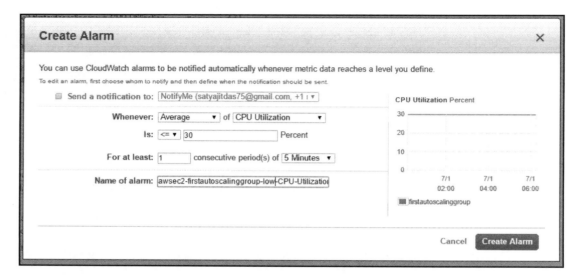

Alarm for decrease group size

7. Put the number of instances to be added and removed when the respective policies occur. Click on **Review**:

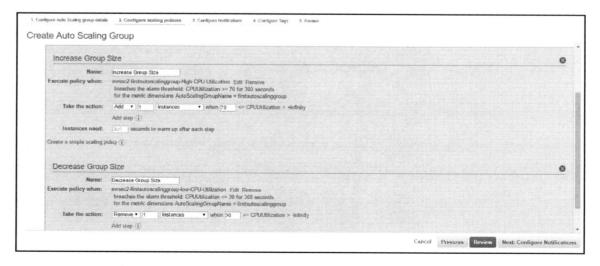

Configure scaling policy for Auto Scaling group

8. Review the details and click on **Create Auto Scaling group**:

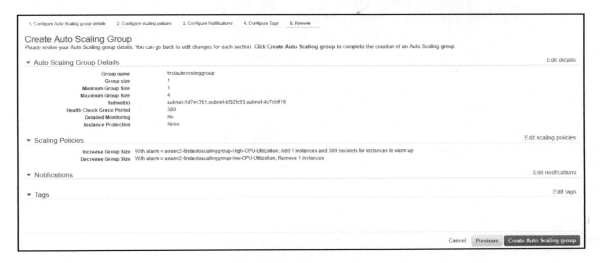

Review creation of Auto Scaling group

9. An Auto Scaling group will be created and the next time you go to the menu, you will see the newly created Auto Scaling group:

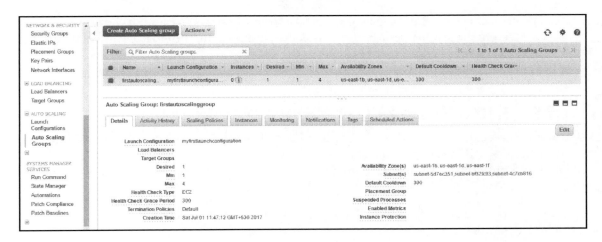

Auto Scaling group details

10. Note that one instance will be created and the instances column will show **1** after some time. Even if you delete the instance, one more instance will be created to have the minimum number of instances defined in this group. If you want to associate the Auto Scaling group with a load balancer, click on the **Edit** button on the **Details** tab. Add the load balancer and the target group. Click on the **Save** button:

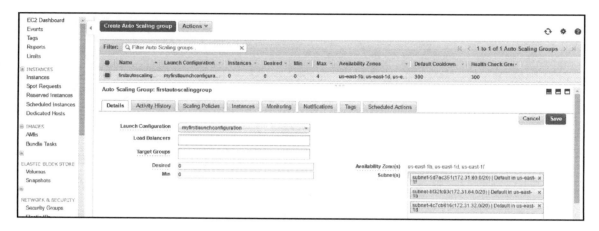

Edit Auto Scaling group details

11. You can select the Auto Scaling group from the **Actions** menu to **Edit** or **Delete** the scaling group. If you delete a scaling group, instances associated with this group will also be terminated.

# There's more...

Scaling policies can be defined using any available cloud watch statistics. We can define the custom cloud watch metrics which can also be used to define policies. If you define the desired and minimum instance as 0, instances will not be created even if you don't delete the scaling group.

You can define the scheduled actions if you want the number of instances to vary according to a fixed schedule.

# Creating VPC peering

Instances in a VPC are isolated from other VPCs. We need to create VPC peering to communicate between instances using the private IPv4 or IPv6 IPs. You can create peering between two VPCs in the same region. Both the VPCs can either belong to the same AWS account or different accounts. Here we'll learn how to create VPC peering between two VPCs in one account.

## Getting ready

Log in to the console with the appropriate permissions.

## How to do it...

The steps to create VPC peering are as follows:

1. Browse to the AWS VPC console. In the left menu option, choose **Peering Connections** under **Virtual Private Cloud**:

Create Peering Connection

2. Click on **Create Peering Connection**. Provide the **Peering connection name tag, VPC (Requester)** and **VPC (Accepter)**. Click on **Create Peering Connection**:

Creating Peering Connection

3. In the dashboard, you can see the created peering connection. However the status is **Pending Acceptance**:

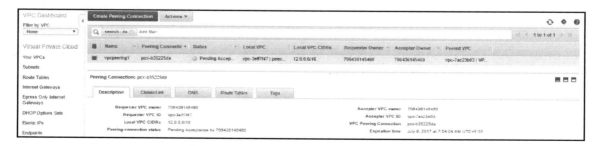

Dashboard with Peering Connection Created

# Accepting VPC peering

Peering is not complete till the owner of the accepter VPC accepts the peering request. Also, you need to enable the Route Table of the VPC to enable network traffic flow.

## Getting ready

Log in to the console with the appropriate permissions. The recipe for *Creating VPC peering* has to be executed first.

## How to do it...

The steps for accepting VPC peering:

1. Browse to the AWS VPC console. In the left menu option, choose **Peering Connections** under **Virtual Private Cloud**. Select the peering connection and browse to **Actions** | **Accept Request**:

Peering Connection Actions

2. The following window will open. Click on **Yes, Accept**. The confirmation window will come with an option to **Modify my route tables now;** you can click that to go to the Route Tables page. We'll choose **Close** and do this later:

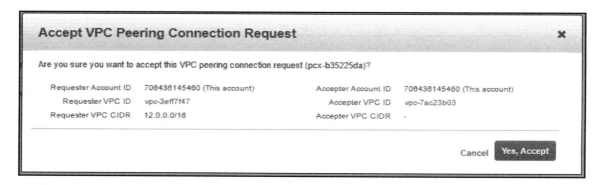

Accept Peering Connection Request

3. You can see the status has now changed to **Active**:

4. Browse to **Actions** | **Edit DNS Settings**. Allow the DNS resolution. Click on the **Save** button:

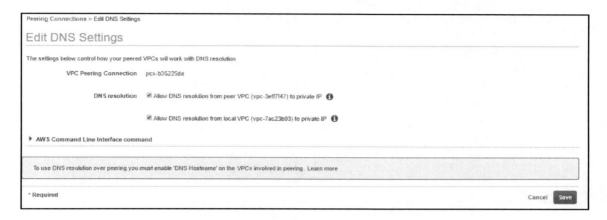

DNS setting of Peering Connection

5. You can see that the DNS settings are now enabled. To delete the peering connection, choose **Actions** | **Delete VPC Peering Connection**:

Peering Connection Details

6. Go to the VPC associated with the peering connection. Click on the Route Table of one VPC. Click on the **Edit** button and add the route for VPC peering mentioning the CIDR range of other VPCs as shown. Click on the **Save** button. Do the same for the other VPC routing table:

Routing for VPC with Peering Connection

7. Now you are ready and the instances of one VPC can communicate with the other VPC peering connection.

# There's more...

You may get an error in the last step when mentioning VPC does not have a public hostname enabled. Select the respective VPC from the VPC console. From **Actions** | **Edit DNS Hostname**, select **yes** and save. Try again and configure VPC Peering.

# Configuring routes between multiple VPCs peered together

For allowing communication between multiple VPCs, you need to create a peering connection between each participating VPC individually. If there are three VPCs, A, B, and C and you want to create a peering connection then you need to create the connection, A-B, B-C and A-C.

# Limitations of VPC peering connection

Limitations of VPC peering connection are:

- You cannot create a peering connection between VPCs with an overlapping CIDR range.
- You cannot create VPC peering between VPCs in different regions.
- Peering does not support unicast reverse path forwarding.
- Peering is not transitive. This means, if you have peering between VPC A and B, and you also have another peering between A and C, A and C cannot talk to each other.

# Controlling access to VPC peering connections

VPC peering connections can't be created or modified by IAM users by default. An IAM policy allowing VPC peering connections needs to be created and added to an IAM group. Users who need to manage peering connections need to be added to the group.

# Configuring VPN connections to your Amazon VPC

By default, instances in your data center cannot communicate securely to instances in the VPC. Establishing an IPSec VPN enables you to do so. There are three components of a VPN connection which are as follows:

- **Virtual Private Gateway (VGW)** is a part of the VPN connection on the AWS side. AWS provides two redundant IPSec tunnels in the VPC to provide high availability.
- **Customer Gateway (CGW)** is a part of the VPN connection on the data center. To have redundant connections for high availability, we need multiple CGWs configured in the data center. It will ensure continuous connectivity, even if one fails.
- VPN connection that connects between VGW and CGW.

To have connectivity to multiple data centers, you need to configure different CGWs and configure the VPN channel with the same VGW:

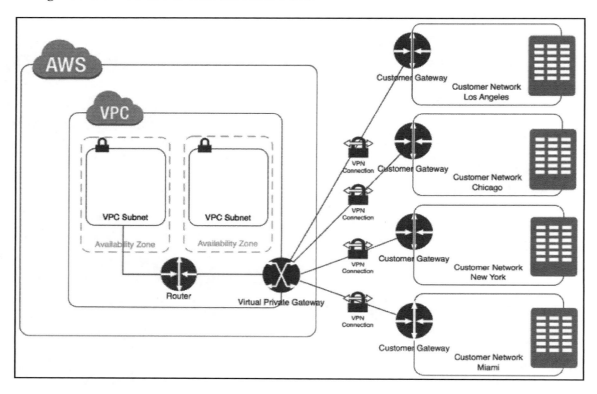

Multiple VPN Connection with VPC

Source:
http://docs.aws.amazon.com/AmazonVPC/latest/UserGuide/images/Branch_Offices_
diagram.png

# Getting ready

Log in to the console with the appropriate permissions.

# How to do it...

The steps are as follows:

1. Browse to the VPC console. Select the **Virtual Private Gateways** option under the **VPN Connections** on the left menu. Click on **Create Virtual Private Gateway**:

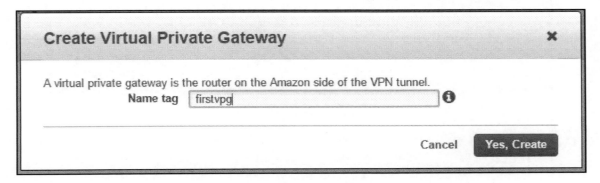

Create Virtual Private Gateway

2. Provide the **Name tag** and you can click on **Yes, Create**. You can see the **State** as **detached**:

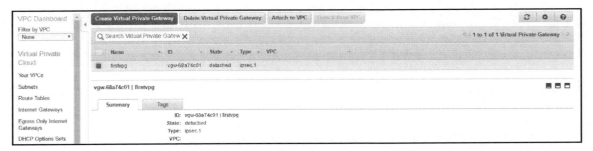

Virtual private gateway created and detached

3. Click on **Attach to VPC**. Select the VPC with which you want to attach the VGW. Click on **Yes, Attach**:

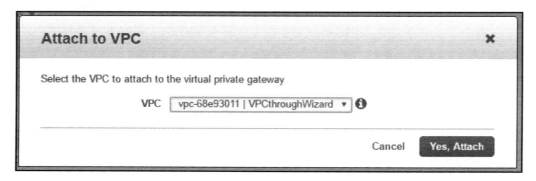

Attaching Virtual Private Gateway to VPC

4. You can see that the **state** has changed to **attached** after some time. Also, the VPC with which it is attached is shown in detail. If you want to delete a VPG, you need to first detach it and then delete it from the top menu options:

Virtual Private Gateway Created and Attached

5. Select the **Virtual Private Gateways** option under **VPN Connections** on the left menu. Click on **Create Customer Gateway**. Provide the **Name tag** and **IP address**, leave **Routing** as **Static**. Click on **Yes, Create**:

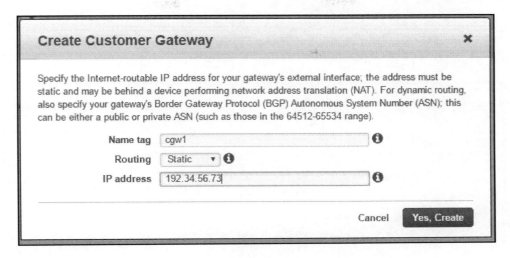

Create customer gateway

6. You can see the CGW that we created with **Status available**. You can delete the CGW by clicking the **Delete Customer Gateway** button when you no longer need it:

Customer Gateway Details

7. Click on **VPN Connections** from the left menu option and click on **Create VPN Connection**. Provide the **Name tag,** choose the **Virtual Private Gateway,** **Customer Gateway**, and click on **Yes, Create**:

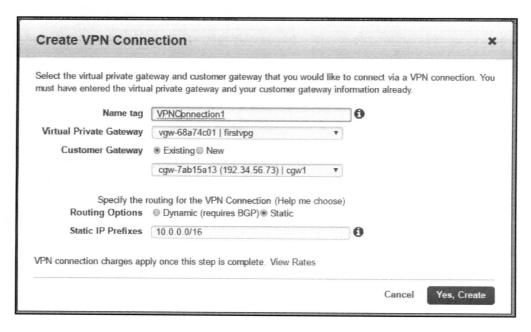

Create VPN connection

8. You can see the VPN connection created in the dashboard. You can remove the VPN by clicking the **Delete** button when you don't need it:

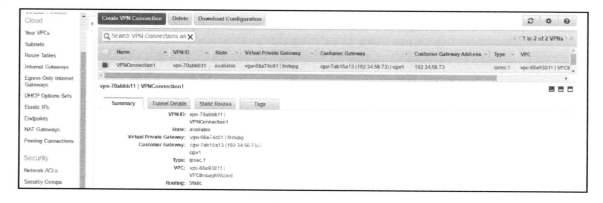

VPN connection details

9. Click on **Download Configuration**. You can choose the **Vendor, Platform,** and **Software** in the window. For now, let's choose **Microsoft** as the **Vendor, Windows Server** as the **Platform,** and **2012 R2** as the **Software**. Click on **Yes, Download** to download the configuration file for configuring the router in DC.

The content of the file will be like the following:

```
! Amazon Web Services
! Virtual Private Cloud
! To configure this VPN connection using the New Connection
Security Rule Wizard
! in the Windows Server 2012 R2 console, use the information below
and refer to
! the AWS VPC Network Administrator Guide for more information:
!
http://docs.aws.amazon.com/AmazonVPC/latest/NetworkAdminGuide/custo
mer-gateway-windows-2012.html
! Your VPN Connection ID               : vpn-70abbb11
! Your Virtual Private Gateway ID        : vgw-68a74c01
! Your Customer Gateway ID             : cgw-7ab15a13
! Information needed for the configuration of your VPN connection:
! vgw-68a74c01 Tunnel1
! ------------------------------------------------------------
----------------
! Local Tunnel Endpoint:           192.34.56.73
! Remote Tunnel Endpoint:          34.225.227.231
! Endpoint 1:                      [Your_Static_Route_IP_Prefix]
! Endpoint 2:                      [Your_VPC_CIDR_Block]
! Preshared key:                   yM2c0CIQsERVaVPHLPP97zt7NMw0U7tu
! vgw-68a74c01 Tunnel2
! ------------------------------------------------------------
----------------
! Local Tunnel Endpoint:           192.34.56.73
! Remote Tunnel Endpoint:          34.227.145.250
! Endpoint 1:                      [Your_Static_Route_IP_Prefix]
! Endpoint 2:                      [Your_VPC_CIDR_Block]
! Preshared key:                   jmTUcawwqCh1hs0aPMTdu1kAIhLYOSF2
! Local Tunnel Endpoint:
! The IP address you entered for your customer gateway when you
created
! the VPN connection for your Amazon VPC.
!
! * You should use the private IP address of the Windows Server
2012 R2
! server rather than this IP address when you enter the Local
Tunnel Endpoint
```

```
! in the New Connection Security Rule Wizard or in the netsh script
below.
! Remote Tunnel Endpoint
! One of two IP addresses for the Amazon virtual private gateway
that
! terminates the VPN connection on the AWS side of the connection.
! Endpoint 1
! The IP prefix that you entered as a static route when you created
your
! VPN connection. This indicates the IP addresses in your network
that are
! allowed to use the VPN connection to access your Amazon VPC.
! Endpoint 2
! The IP address range (CIDR block) of your Amazon VPC; for
example, 10.0.0.0/16
! Preshared key
! This is the pre-shared key that is used to establish IPsec VPN
connection
! between the Local Tunnel Endpoint and the Remote Tunnel Endpoint.
! Note
! From time to time, AWS will perform routine maintenance on the
virtual private
! gateway. This maintenance may disable one of the two tunnels of
your VPN
! connection for a brief period of time. Your VPN connection will
automatically
! fail over to the second tunnel while this maintenance is
performed. To ensure
! uninterrupted service, it's important that you configure both
tunnels.
! Configuration Details for IKE and IPsec
! =========================================
! Additional information regarding the Internet Key Exchange (IKE)
and IPsec
! Security Associations (SA) are presented below. Because the AWS
VPC VPN
! suggested settings are the same as the Windows Server 2012 R2
default IPsec
! configuration settings, minimal work is needed on your part (see
QuickModePFS
! below.)
! MainModeSecMethods:          DHGroup2-AES128-SHA1
! MainModeKeyLifetime:         480min,0sess
! QuickModeSecMethods:         ESP:SHA1-AES128+60min+100000kb
! QuickModePFS:                DHGroup2
! MainModeSecMethods
! This specifies the encryption and authentication algorithms for
the IKE SA.
```

```
! These are the suggested settings for the AWS VPC VPN connection and are the
! default settings for Windows Server 2012 R2 IPsec VPN connections.
! MainModeKeyLifetime
! This specifies the IKE SA key lifetime.  This is the suggested setting for
! the AWS VPC VPN connection and is the default setting for Windows Server
! 2012 R2 IPsec VPN connections.
! QuickModeSecMethods
! This specifies the encryption and authentication algorithms for the IPsec SA.
! These are the suggested settings for the AWS VPC VPN connection and are the
! default settings for Windows Server 2012 R2 IPsec VPN connections.
! QuickModePFS
! The use of master key perfect forward secrecy (PFS) is suggested for your
! IPsec sessions. Enabling PFS isn't possible via the Windows Server 2012 R2
! user interface. The only way to enable this setting is to execute the netsh
! script (below) with QMPFS=dhgroup2
! Dead Gateway Detection
! -------------------------------------------------------------------------------
! To configure TCP to detect when a gateway becomes unavailable, run the following
! command to enable Dead Gateway Detection:
reg add HKLM\System\CurrentControlSet\services\Tcpip\Parameters ^
/v EnableDeadGWDetect /t REG_DWORD /d 1
! After you change the registry key, you must reboot the server.
! Netsh script to configure your IPsec VPN connection
! -------------------------------------------------------------------------------
! You can automatically configure your IPsec VPN connection by copying and pasting
! the netsh scripts below. Replace the items in brackets [] with the appropriate
! values as indicated above.
! Script for Tunnel 1:
netsh advfirewall consec add rule Name="vgw-68a74c01 Tunnel 1" ^
Enable=Yes Profile=any Type=Static Mode=Tunnel ^
LocalTunnelEndpoint=[Windows_Server_Private_IP_address] ^
RemoteTunnelEndpoint=34.225.227.231
Endpoint1=[Your_Static_Route_IP_Prefix] ^
```

```
Endpoint2=[Your_VPC_CIDR_Block] Protocol=Any
Action=RequireInClearOut ^
Auth1=ComputerPSK Auth1PSK=yM2cOCIQsERVaVPHLPP97zt7NMw0U7tu ^
QMSecMethods=ESP:SHA1-AES128+60min+100000kb ^
ExemptIPsecProtectedConnections=No ApplyAuthz=No QMPFS=dhgroup2
! Script for Tunnel 2:
netsh advfirewall consec add rule Name="vgw-68a74c01 Tunnel 2" ^
Enable=Yes Profile=any Type=Static Mode=Tunnel ^
LocalTunnelEndpoint=[Windows_Server_Private_IP_address] ^
RemoteTunnelEndpoint=34.227.145.250
Endpoint1=[Your_Static_Route_IP_Prefix] ^
Endpoint2=[Your_VPC_CIDR_Block] Protocol=Any
Action=RequireInClearOut ^
Auth1=ComputerPSK Auth1PSK=jmTUcawwqCh1hs0aPMTdu1kAIhLYOSF2 ^
QMSecMethods=ESP:SHA1-AES128+60min+100000kb ^
ExemptIPsecProtectedConnections=No ApplyAuthz=No QMPFS=dhgroup2
! Additional Notes and Questions
!   - Amazon Virtual Private Cloud Getting Started Guide:
!
http://docs.aws.amazon.com/AmazonVPC/latest/GettingStartedGuide
!   - Amazon Virtual Private Cloud Network Administrator Guide:
!
http://docs.aws.amazon.com/AmazonVPC/latest/NetworkAdminGuide
!   - XSL Version: 2009-07-15-1119716
```

You configure the router in your data center with this configuration. You are all set for primitively connecting AWS from your data center.

# 4

# Configuring Global Scale Infrastructure

In this chapter, we will learn the following recipes:

- Creating a VPC and Subnet from the CLI
- Creating a VPC to DC Connectivity--VPN Tunneling
- Creating a VPC with a private subnet and connecting DC
- Creating a multi-region VPC communication
- Setting up a private DNS with a VPC
- Migrating to IPv6

## Introduction

In this chapter, we will learn how to quickly create different AWS VPC networking topologies. We will also learn how to connect two VPCs in the same region or across different AWS regions. Criteria for choosing one of the different available topologies of VPC will depend on the following different considerations:

- **Availability of the application deployed to AWS**: Single AZ deployment can provide moderate availability. Multi AZ deployments will provide high availability and fault tolerance of a single AZ failure. Multi region deployment will provide very high availability of the application. It will be available even if the complete region of AWS fails.

- **Creating a public and private subnet**: Public and private subnets need to be created based on the security requirements of different layers of the application.
- **Connectivity requirement between data center (DC) and AWS Cloud**: For securely connecting DC and AWS Cloud, VPN needs to be created. However it works over internet. For high bandwidth and dedicated connectivity, direct connect can be configured. VPN hub can be created for connecting multiple DCs to AWS VPCs.
- **Connectivity amongst different VPCs**: Different VPCs in the same or different regions may need to be connected for security and high availability.

AWS provides a VPC wizard for the quick creation of some of these topologies to fit their exact use case.

# Creating a VPC and subnet from the CLI

AWS CLI is a command-line interface that facilitates managing AWS resources from the command line. Until now we have learnt recipes for creating AWS networking components from the console. In this recipe we'll learn how to create them through the CLI. This will help you understand how scripts can be written to automate the management of network components.

## Getting ready

You will need to configure the CLI in your system from which you are going to execute the commands.

## How to do it...

Follow the steps provided to create AWS VPC and subnet from CLI.

1. Open your command prompt and give the command:

```
aws ec2 create-vpc --profile user2 --region us-east-1 --cidr-block
10.0.0.0/16 --amazon-provided-ipv6-cidr-block
```

The different components of our command are explained as follows:

- `aws ec2 create-vpc`: It is the command for creating a VPC profile.
- `user2`: It is the user profile with which a VPC is being created. You may omit this if you want to create the VPC with a default profile.
- `region us-east-1`: It is the AWS region where the VPC is going to be created. You can omit this if you want to create it in the default region.
- `cidr-block 10.0.0.0/16`: It is the IPv4 CIDR block associated with the VPC.
- `amazon-provided-ipv6-cidr-block`: It is an option, if you want AWS to associate IPv6 to be with VPC.

```
D:\>aws ec2 create-vpc --profile user2 --region us-east-1 --cidr-block 10.0.0.0/16 --amazon-provided-ipv6-cidr-block
{
    "Vpc": {
        "VpcId": "vpc-23e0795a",
        "InstanceTenancy": "default",
        "Tags": [],
        "Ipv6CidrBlockAssociationSet": [
            {
                "Ipv6CidrBlock": "",
                "AssociationId": "vpc-cidr-assoc-039f0b68",
                "Ipv6CidrBlockState": {
                    "State": "associating"
                }
            }
        ],
        "State": "pending",
        "DhcpOptionsId": "dopt-ad975ccb",
        "CidrBlock": "10.0.0.0/16",
        "IsDefault": false
    }
}
```

Create VPC from CLI

2. You can see the response where a VPC is created with the ID `vpc-23e0795a` with a given CIDR range for both IPv4 and IPv6.

3. You can browse to the AWS console for the VPC and check that the VPC has been created with the properties shown in the command prompt.

View VPC created from CLI

4. Now let's create a subnet in the VPC by giving the following command:

```
aws ec2 create-subnet --profile user2 --region us-east-1 --vpc-id
vpc-23e0795a --cidr-block 10.0.1.0/24 --ipv6-cidr-block
2600:1f18:4659:5c00::/64
```

Here we are providing the profile and region that we explained earlier. We are also providing the following options:

- `vpc-id vpc-23e0795a`: The VPC in which subnet will be created
- `cidr-block 10.0.1.0/24`: The IPv4 CIDR range of the subnet
- `ipv6-cidr-block 2600:1f18:4659:5c00::/64`: The IPv6 IP range associated with the subnet

```
D:\>aws ec2 create-subnet --profile user2 --region us-east-1 --vpc-id vpc-23e0795a --cidr-block 10.0.1.0/24 --ipv6-cid
r-block 2600:1f18:4659:5c00::/64
{
    "Subnet": {
        "VpcId": "vpc-23e0795a",
        "AvailableIpAddressCount": 251,
        "MapPublicIpOnLaunch": false,
        "DefaultForAz": false,
        "Ipv6CidrBlockAssociationSet": [
            {
                "Ipv6CidrBlock": "2600:1f18:4659:5c00::/64",
                "AssociationId": "subnet-cidr-assoc-96133cdc",
                "Ipv6CidrBlockState": {
                    "State": "associating"
                }
            }
        ],
        "State": "pending",
        "AvailabilityZone": "us-east-1c",
        "SubnetId": "subnet-446b230c",
        "CidrBlock": "10.0.1.0/24",
        "AssignIpv6AddressOnCreation": false
    }
}
D:\>
```

Create subnet from CLI

5. We can browse to the AWS VPC console and go to subnets. We can see the subnet created as shown in the following screenshot:

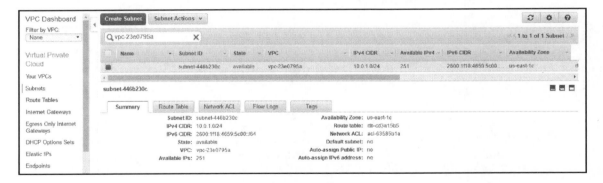

View subnet created from CLI

# There's more...

Hence, you can create multiple VPCs and subnets in multiple regions from a single script. There are multiple other third party tools like Terraform, Chef, Ansible through which you can also create and manage AWS components. You can also use AWS CloudFormation for the same. We will look at some of these in next chapters.

# Creating a VPC to DC connectivity--VPN Tunneling

Earlier we learnt how to create a VPC, subnet and a VPN in separate recipes. In this recipe, we will learn how to create those in a single recipe.

## Getting ready

Log in to your AWS account with the proper permissions for creating the required components.

## How to do it...

AWS provides simple steps for creating basic AWS networking components for first time users.

1. Open the VPC dashboard by browsing `https://console.aws.amazon.com/vpc` as shown in the following screenshot:

VPC console

2. Click on **Start VPC Wizard**. We have already provided a recipe for the first option in `Chapter 1`, *Getting Started with AWS Networking Components*. The following window will open:

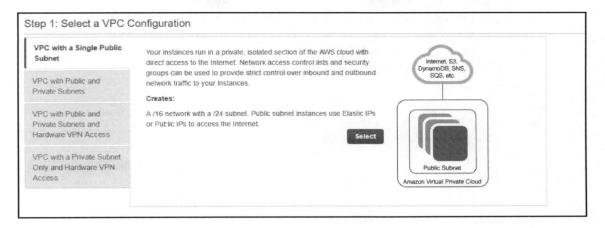

VPC wizard with single public subnet

3. Let's select the option **VPC with Public and Private Subnets and Hardware VPN Access**. The preceding screenshot explains the components that we are going to create.

    - One VPC
    - One public subnet that can be accessed from the internet
    - One private subnet that can be accessed through a corporate data center
    - One VPN connection that connects the corporate data center to the AWS subnet
    - Service endpoint for connecting services like S3 over a private network

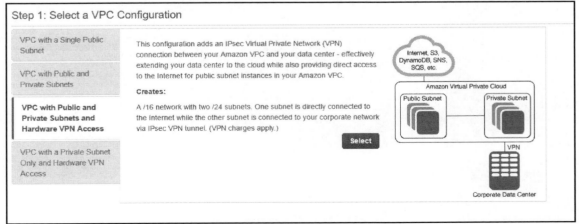

VPC wizard with single public, private subnet, and VPN

4. Click on the **Select** button. Provide the **IPv4 CIDR block, IPv6 CIDR block, VPC name, Public subnet's IPv4 CIDR, Availability Zone** for the public subnet, **Public subnet name, Private subnet's IPv4 CIDR, Availability Zone** for the private subnet, and the **Private subnet name** as shown in the following screenshot:

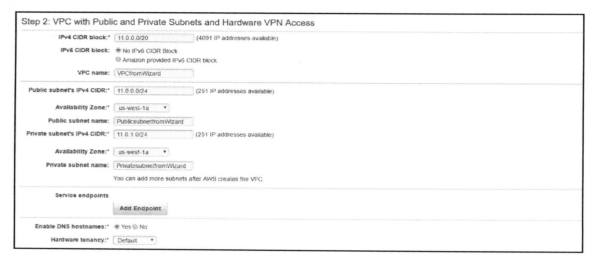

Create VPC, two subnets, and VPN

5. Click on **Add Endpoint**. You can choose the subnet to which the endpoint needs to be connected, and access the policy for either full access or customized access. You can add more endpoints by clicking **Add Endpoint** for attaching multiple endpoints with multiple policies for the target subnet group.

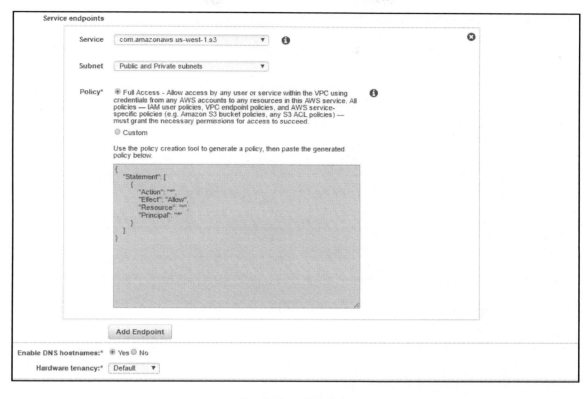

Figure 4- 9 Create a VPC endpoint

6. Choose **Enable DNS hostnames** and **Hardware tenancy**. Click on **Next**.
7. Provide the details for the VPN, and click on **Create VPC**.

VPN configuration

8. You can browse to the **VPC Dashboard** and find the VPC that we created.

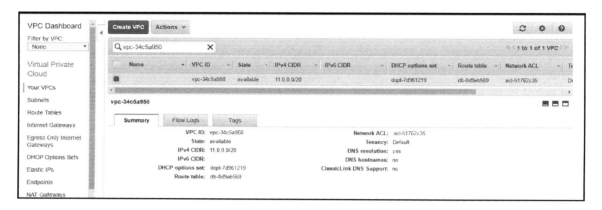

Details of the VPC created

9. You can also see the subnets created and associated with the VPC.

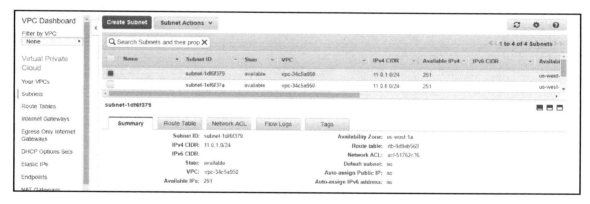

Subnets of VPC created

10. You can also see the VPN connection created and associated with the VPC.

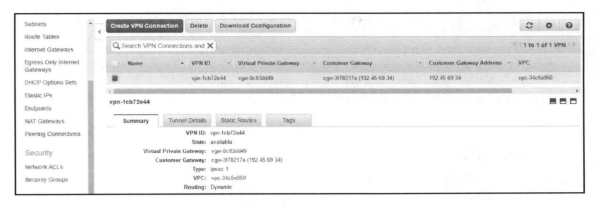

Subnet with the VPC created

11. You can click on **Download Configuration,** and download the configuration file after choosing the right options.

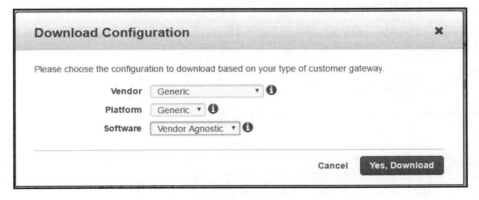

VPN configuration download

# There's more...

In the preceding configuration, NAT is not attached to the routes created with the public subnet. So if instances want to have internet connectivity, they can either do that through the DC network or an additional NAT needs to be attached. Instances in a public subnet can access DC either through the internet or through the VPN.

# Creating a VPC with a private subnet and connecting DC

Sometimes for security purposes, you will want to host instances in AWS and treat it as an extension of the corporate DC. In this case, VPC will only have a private subnet and a VPN connection to the DC for connectivity. In this recipe, we will learn how to create connectivity with the DC, without creating a public subnet.

## Getting ready

Log in to your AWS account with proper permissions for creating the required components.

## How to do it...

1. Open the VPC dashboard by browsing to `https://console.aws.amazon.com/vpc` as shown in the following screenshot:

VPC wizard

2. Click on **Start VPC Wizard**. Let's select the option **VPC with a Private Subnet Only and Hardware VPN Access**. The screenshot explains the components that we are going to create.
    - One VPC
    - One private subnet that can be accessed through a corporate data center
    - One VPN connection that connects the corporate data center to the AWS subnet
    - Service endpoint for connecting services like S3 over a private network

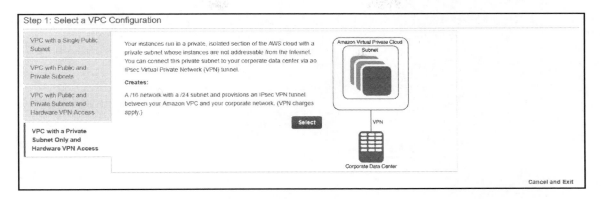

VPC wizard with Private Subnet and Hardware VPN

3. Click on the **Select** button. Provide the required details. You can optionally click on **Add Endpoint**. Click on **Next**.

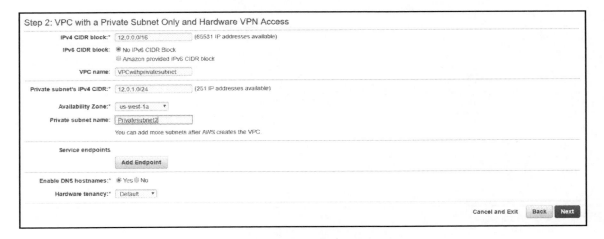

Details of private subnet and hardware VPN

4. Provide the required details for a VPN connection. Click on **Create VPC** as shown in the following screenshot:

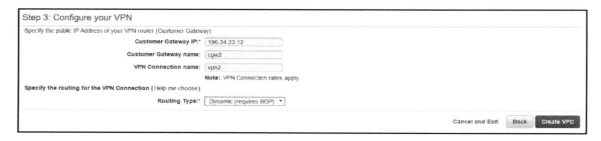

Configure VPN

5. Provide the required details for a VPN connection. Click on **Create VPC**. The VPC will be created. You can then browse to the **VPC Dashboard** to see the details of the VPC as shown in the following screenshot:

Details of VPC created

# Creating a multi-region VPC communication

Sometimes we need to host applications across multiple VPCs that spread across several regions for hosting a solution in very high demand. In this case, we need to have connectivity between VPCs in different regions. There are multiple options for how this can be achieved. We'll do this using the **strongSwan** open source software which is an implementation of the IPSEC-based VPN solution.

## Getting ready

Log in to your AWS account with proper permissions for creating the required components.

## How to do it...

1. Create a VPC from the VPC wizard in the **US-West (Oregon)** region using the **VPC with a Single Public Subnet** option with CIDR range 7.0.0.0/16 for VPC and 7.0.0.0/24 for the subnet as shown in the following screenshot:

VPC creation in one region

2. Create another VPC from the VPC wizard in the **US-East (Ohio)** region using the **VPC with a Single Public Subnet** option with CIDR range `8.0.0.0/16` for VPC and `8.0.0.0/24` for the subnet as shown in the following screenshot:

VPC creation in second region

3. Change the region to **US-West (Oregon)**. Create an EC2 instance in the first region using an AMI for an Ubuntu Server, `t2.micro` instance type to VPC and the subnet that we created. Configure the security group for allowing traffic for the following:

- TCP 22 (SSH protocol) from `0.0.0.0/0`
- UDP 500 (IKE protocol) from `0.0.0.0/0`
- UDP 4500 (IPSec/UDP) from `0.0.0.0/0`
- All TCP from `8.0.0.0/16` (second VPC)

Note that you should configure the SG based on your requirements. Also create and store the key.

The EC2 will look like the following from the console:

Details of EC2 created in one region

4. Disable source destination and check for the instance.

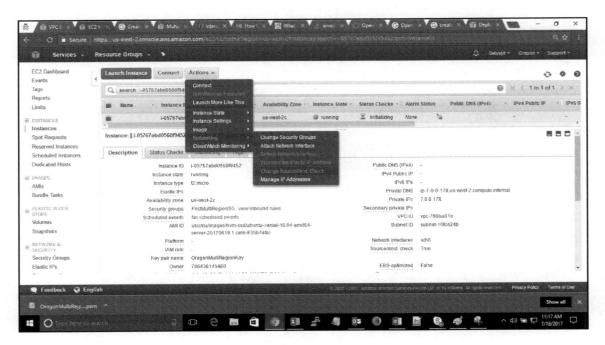

Disabling source destination Check for EC2

5. Attach an elastic IP to the instance. It has a public IP attached to it as shown in the following screenshot:

Attach Elastic IP to one instance

6. Create a similar instance in the **US-East (Ohio)** region in the VPC and in the subnet that we created. Disable source-destination check. Attach the Elastic IP. The only difference from step 3 is to assign security groups for allowing traffic from the first VPC:

- TCP 22 (SSH protocol) from `0.0.0.0/0`
- UDP 500 (IKE protocol) from `0.0.0.0/0`
- UDP 4500 (IPSec/UDP) from `0.0.0.0/0`
- All TCP from `7.0.0.0/16` (first VPC)

It should look like the following:

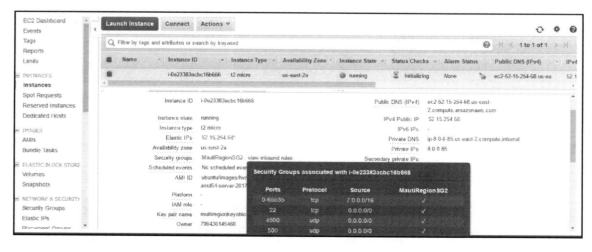

EC2 details in second region

7. Log in to an instance in the **Ohio** region by following the earlier recipe. The default log in name is `ubuntu`.

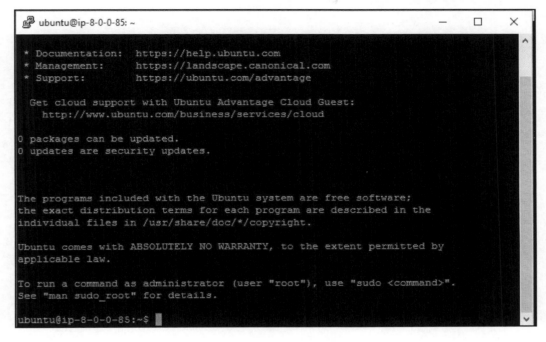

Log in to EC2 in one region

8. To enable packet forwarding in the instance, execute the following command:

```
sudo sysctl -w net.ipv4.ip_forward=1
```

```
ubuntu@ip-8-0-0-85:~$ sudo sysctl -w net.ipv4.ip_forward=1
net.ipv4.ip_forward = 1
```

Figure 4- 27 Configure IPv4 forward

9. Install `strongswan` in your instance using the following command:

```
sudo apt-get install -y strongswan
```

We need to configure the `/etc/strongswan/ipsec.conf` file for setting up a connection. This needs to be put in the EC2 instances of both regions. Here is the common part for each:

```
config setup
strictcrlpolicy=no
charondebug=all
conn %default
ikelifetime=60m
keylife=20m
rekeymargin=3m
keyingtries=1
keyexchange=ikev2
```

This additional section needs to be put in the EC2 instance of `Ohio` region:

```
conn Ohio
authby=secret
auto=start
type=tunnel
left=8.0.0.85
leftid=52.15.254.68
leftsubnet=8.0.0.0/16
leftauth=psk
right=54.148.58.245
rightsubnet=7.0.0.0/16
rightauth=psk
ike=aes128-sha1-modp1024
esp=aes128-sha1-modp1024
```

This additional section needs to be put in the EC2 instance of `Oregon` region:

```
conn Oregon
authby=secret
auto=start
type=tunnel
left=7.0.0.178
leftid=54.148.58.245
leftsubnet=7.0.0.0/16
leftauth=psk
right=52.15.254.68
rightsubnet=8.0.0.0/16
rightauth=psk
ike=aes128-sha1-modp1024
esp=aes128-sha1-modp1024
```

Create and save the files with your favorite text editor. You can see that the left side represents the IP and CIDR of the EC2 and VPC of the same AWS region the EC2 is being configured. The right side has the details for the other EC2 and VPC of the other AWS region.

10. Create a `/etc/strongswan/ipsec.secrets` file with your favourite editor with content like the following in both instances. Change the public IP and secret key as per your case.

```
<local public ip> : PSK "your key"
<foreign public ip> : PSK "your key "
```

11. Add the following line to the `/etc/sysctl.conf` file in both the EC2 instances.

**`net.ipv4.ip_forward=1`**

12. Run the following command in both instances:

**`sysctl -p`**

13. Go to the routing table attached to the subnet which we created, and add the destination route of the other VPC CIDR and target it as the instance ID which we created.

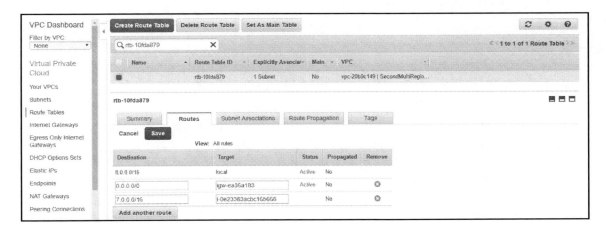

Configure Route Table for one region

14. Do the same for the routing table for other regions as well.

Configure Route Table for second region

15. Now execute the following command to start strongswan as a root user:

```
service. strongswan start
```

16. To check the status of the connection, execute the following command:

```
service strongswan status
```

# There's more...

You can ping one server in one region from other server in other region for checking connectivity between EC2 of both regions.

You should opt for stronger security policies for production use case. For example, the security groups should be open to a specific IP address range or the passphrase should be stronger.

# Setting up a private DNS with a VPC

Route 53 is a very highly available DNS server in AWS. It can work for both external routing as well as internal routing. Internal routing works within the internal network of a VPC where both source and destination services can be connected via internal IPs. It can be used for users or applications to connect within the private network boundary. The private network can be extended to Corporate data center, other VPC in same region connected through VPC peering or VPC in other region connected privately over secure channel.

## Getting ready

Log in to your AWS account with proper permissions for creating the required components.

## How to do it...

1. Browse to the VPC console and select the VPC in which you want to configure the private DNS. Check if the **DNS resolution** and **DNS Hostnames** are **yes** as shown in the following screesnhot:

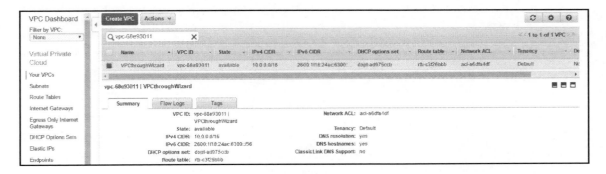

Check VPC DNS resolution and DNS hostnames

2. Browse to `https://console.aws.amazon.com/route53/home`, to go to the Route 53 home page. You will see in the following page that you don't have any DNS configured yet:

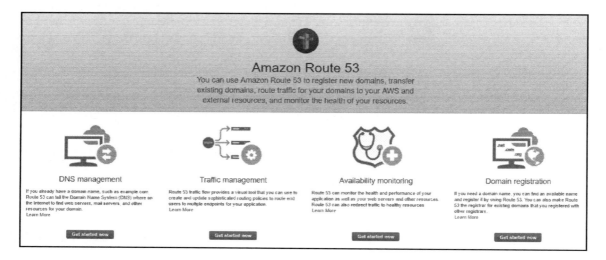

AWS Route 53 dashboard

3. Click on **Get started now** under **DNS management**. The following window will appear:

Create hosted zone

4. Click on **Create Hosted Zone**. Provide a **Domain Name** and **Comment**. In the **Type** drop down choose **Private Hosted Zone for Amazon VPC**. Select the **VPC ID** where this service will be configured. Click on the **Create** button as you can see in the following screenshot:

Hosted zone details

5. You will see the default record set associated with this DNS. You can also select the record set and change properties.

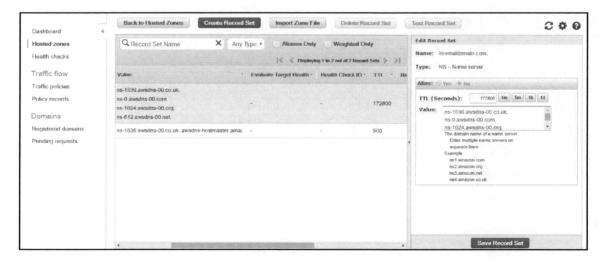

AWS record set details

6. You can click on **Create Record Set** to click additional record sets if required. Provide the **Name**, choose the **Type** and the routing policy as required. Provide a **TTL (Seconds)** and **Value**. Click on **Create**. I have selected **Type** as **A - IPv4 addresses**. I have provided internal IP of EC2 instances which I created earlier as you can see in the following screenshot:

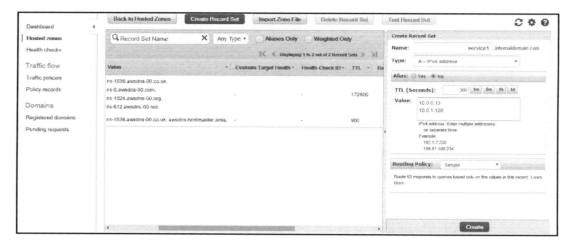

Create record set

7. You can see the record set created in the following screenshot:

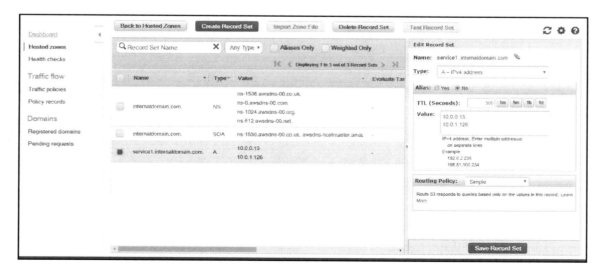

Custom record set details for record A

8. You can see the hosted zone created by selecting the **Hosted Zones** on the menu on the left.

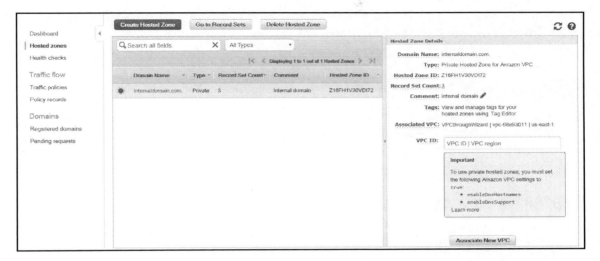

Hosted zone created

9. You can add the required VPC by clicking on the **Associate New VPC** button and selecting the VPC to be associated.

10. If you want to configure the internal domain forwarding requests to elb, the same steps should be followed, only the record **Type** should be CNAME and the **Value** is elb DNS name as you can see in the following screenshot:

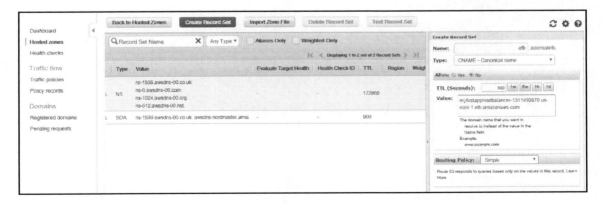

Record set for ELB CNAME record

# There's more...

DNS hostname and DNS support needs to be enabled for the VPC where you are going to configure the private DNS. By default, these are enabled; otherwise you can do that from the **Actions** drop-down after selecting the VPC.

# Migrating to IPv6

IPv6 support has been added to AWS since December 2016. So VPCs created prior to that didn't have IPv6 support. This recipe shows how to add IPv6 support with VPCs that have been created with the IPv4 option only.

# Getting ready

Log in to your AWS account with proper permissions for creating the required components.

# How to do it...

1. Open the VPC dashboard by browsing to `https://console.aws.amazon.com/vpc`. Select the VPC without IPv6 support. You can see that **IPv6 CIDR** is blank as shown in the following screenshot:

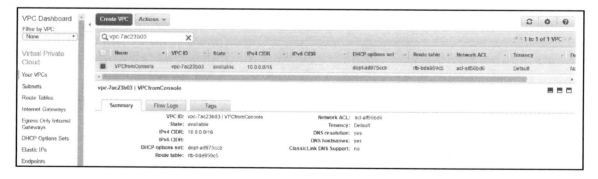

Check VPC IPv6 CIDR

2. Click **Actions | Edit CIDRs**. The following window will open. Click on **Add IPv6 CIDR** button. **IPv6 CIDR** will be associated. Click **Close** as shown in the following screenshot:

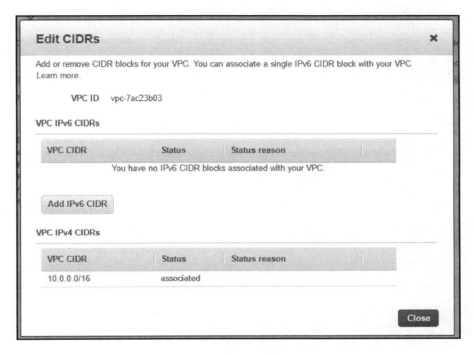

Edit VPC IPv6 CIDR

3. You can see it reflected in the **Summary** as well:

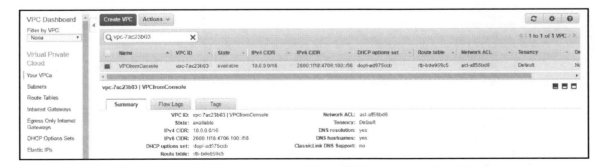

VPC Summary after IPv6 Support

4. Select the subnet associated with the VPC on which you want to enable IPv6 CIDR.

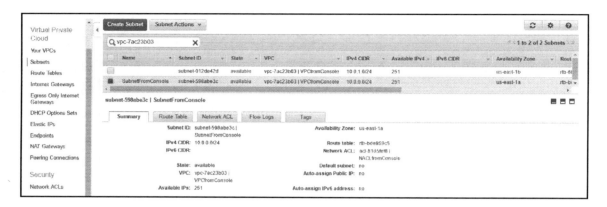

Subnet summary before IPv6 support

5. Click **Subnet Actions** and edit IPv6 CIDR. Click on **Add IPv6 CIDR**. Edit IPv6 CIDR range and click on the tick button. Click on the **Close** button as seen in the following screenshot:

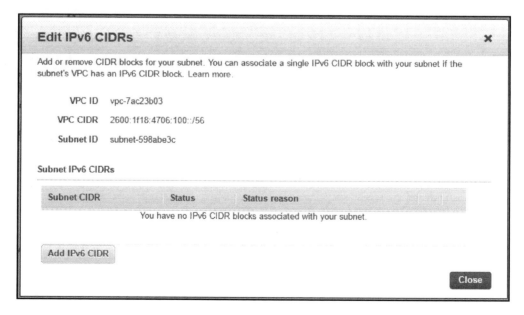

Edit Subnet IPv6 support

6. You can see the IPv6 associated with the subnet from the **Summary** as seen in the following screenshot:

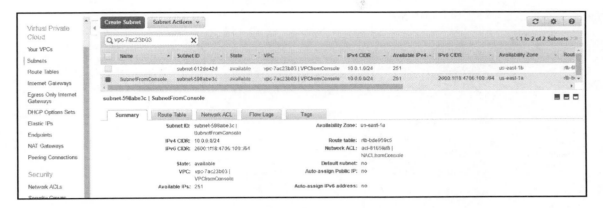

Subnet summary after IPv6 support

7. NAT instances don't work with IPv6 addresses. To enable the egress of traffic from instances hosted in a private subnet, we need an **Egress Only Internet Gateways** to be associated with the routing table. So you need to create an Egress-Only Internet Gateway. Click on **Egress Only Internet Gateways**.

Egress Only Internet Gateway dashboard

8. Click on **Create Egress Only Internet Gateway**. Associate the VPC from the dropdown menu. Click on **Create.**

Create Egress Only Internet Gateway

9. Select the **Routing Tables** from the left menu bar. Select one associated with the private subnet of the VPC. Go to the **Routes** tab. Click on **Edit**. Click on **Add another route**. Put : : / 0 in the destination and select the Internet Gateway in the **Target**. Click on **Save**.

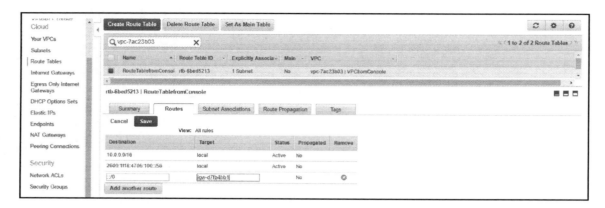

Modify router for IPv6 support

10. Select **Security Group** from the left menu bar. Select one associated with the subnet of the VPC. Go to the **Inbound Rules** tab. Click on **Edit**. Click on **Add another rule**. Put : : / 0 or appropriate IPv6 CIDR range in the source. Click on **Save**.

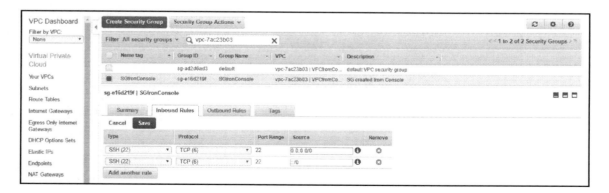

Security Group Support for IPv6

11. If you have modified the default rules of NACL, you also need to add the configuration for IPv6; as we have not done that, we are skipping this step.

12. Finally you need to assign the IPv6 address to the EC2. Browse to the **EC2 Dashboard**. In the menu, choose **Instances**. Select the instance and choose **Actions I Networking I Manage IP Address:**

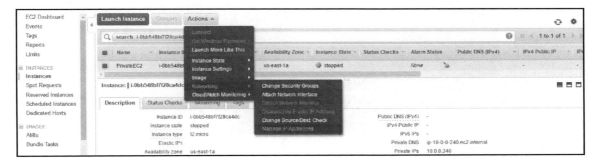

IPv6 support for EC2

13. The following window will open. Click on **Assign New IP** under **IPv6 Addresses**. Click on **Yes, Update**. The IPv6 address will be assigned to instance.

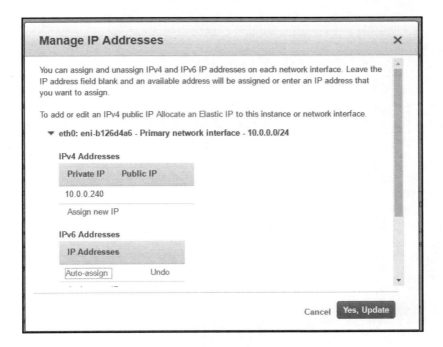

Manage EC2 IPv6 IP

14. The IPv6 address will be assigned to instance. You can see that in the dashboard.

Instance with IPv6 support

# There's more...

All EC2 instance types are not IPv6 compliant. You can't migrate such instances to IPv6. You need to change the instance type to one that is IPv6 compliant before adding support to IPv6.

# 5
# Working with Infrastructure Automation

In this chapter, we will cover the following recipes:

- Creating, storing, and testing the template--CloudFormation
- Creating a new stack--CloudFormation
- Modifying the stack--CloudFormation
- Deleting the stack--CloudFormation
- Setting up Ansible
- Installing Ansible
- Creating Ansible playbooks for creating VPC

## Introduction

Networking infrastructure has become increasingly complex and advanced, and managing the configuration of networks has come under increased demands for higher velocity and consistency.

This chapter will focus on creating basic building blocks, that is, networks using automation scripts. We will be using CloudFormation and Ansible tools for automation. There are sample playbooks for your reference.

CloudFormation provided by AWS gives us the ability to provision and manage AWS resources. CloudFormation templates support a wide range of AWS resources; you can create templates for the services and applications you want to build. You can create or update a stack to provision/manage the resources. You can create a template for managing a single EC2 instance or a highly available multi-tier application. The best part of CloudFormation is it automatically takes care of the sequence required for provisioning resources. There is no additional charge for CloudFormation; you just need to pay for the created resources. It supports YAML and JSON written templates.

Ansible, powered by Red Hat, gives almost the same, and sometimes more, functionalities than other DevOps tools. With Ansible, migrations from anywhere, that is on-premises infrastructure, cloud to AWS, or anywhere become very easy. With Ansible, you can use the same simple playbook `.yaml` language to manage your infrastructure and deploy your application. Redeploy the application to a different environment by just changing the environment parameters.

# Infrastructure as a Service

**Infrastructure as a Service (IaaS)** is one of the service models of cloud computing that outsources computer infrastructure to support infrastructure operations. The basic functioning of IaaS is to allow all the hardware, the rack of servers, storage devices, and the network that is kept in the cloud and lets somebody else use it for their basic functioning.

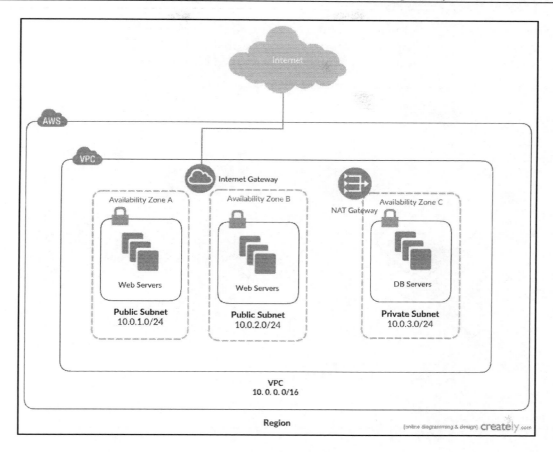

VPC Setup

# Why do we need to automate?

Think of a scenario where you have really spent your blood to make things work and suddenly, one day, you get a message in the middle of the night that one of your regions has an API issue and it has started to affect your business. You have tried recovering that server but nothing seems to be fruitful and now you are forced to build the same infrastructure in another region. It is tough for you to even remember the sequence of the commands and the software that needs to be installed. Automation provides an effortless way of writing a piece of code for everything, from creating the network to making everything up and running.

There are ways in which creating an infrastructure can be automated as per your requirements. Your automation should sense the current region/infrastructure and should directly trigger a new infrastructure in another region in case of any failure.

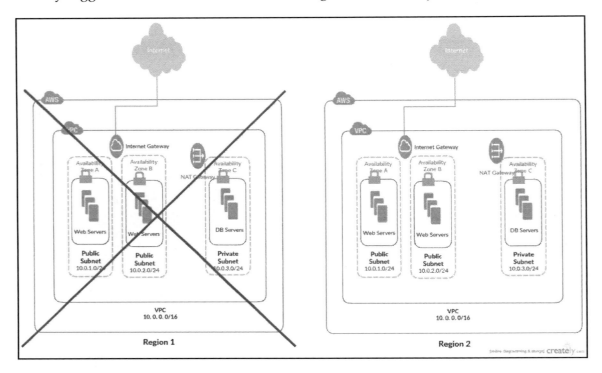

VPC Setup in another region while failure

# Infrastructure automation tools

It always feels good to build an IT infrastructure from scratch, but when you need to do it regularly it's not so great. Sometimes, you are pushing the same commands, building the same type of servers; the easiest way to do it is by automation.

There are many tools available for automation, so there is no best tool that fits every environment; you should select a tool according to your infrastructure, such as Ansible, CloudFormation, Chef, Puppet, SaltStack, Jenkins, and so on.

In our example, we will be working on CloudFormation and Ansible.

# Creating, storing, and testing the template--CloudFormation

CloudFormation supports creating a VPC and its components for the mentioned CIDR block. We will go through the CloudFormation template and an example (JSON).

## Getting ready

Before creating our first stack, we will need to create a template. CloudFormation templates can be written in JSON or YAML format.

Below are the basic snippets of various functions that we will be using in our example.

## How to do it...

In this section, we will focus on creating, storing, and testing the template. Let's start with some snippets of the template.

## Creating the template

You can create a template in any text editor such as notepad and save the file with a `.json` extension.

### VPC

The format for VPC declaration is: `AWS::EC2::VPC`

```
{
"Type" : "AWS::EC2::VPC",
   "Properties" : {
       "CidrBlock" : String,
       "EnableDnsSupport" : Boolean,
       "EnableDnsHostnames" : Boolean,
       "InstanceTenancy" : String,
       "Tags" : [ Resource Tag, ... ]
   }
}
```

| Sr. No | Property | Required | Type | Available values | Default value |
|---|---|---|---|---|---|
| 1 | CIDRBlock | Yes | String | Example: `192.168.0.0/16` | N/A |
| 2 | EnableDnsSupport | No | Boolean | True/False | TRUE |
| 3 | EnableDnsHostnames | No | Boolean | True/False | TRUE |
| 4 | InstanceTenancy | No | String | "default" / "dedicated" | default |
| 5 | Tags | No | String | Key: String Value: String | NA |

Example:

```
{
   "AWSTemplateFormatVersion" : "2010-09-09",
   "Resources" : {
      "VPCTesting" : {
        "Type" : "AWS::EC2::VPC",
        "Properties" : {
           "CidrBlock" : "10.1.0.0/16",
               "EnableDnsSupport" : "false",               "EnableDnsHostnames"
: "false",                "InstanceTenancy" : "dedicated",
 "Tags" : [ {"Key" : "Name", "Value" : "VPC-Dev"} ]
}
}
}
}
```

## Subnet

The format for subnet declaration is:

```
{
"Type" : "AWS::EC2::Subnet",
"Properties" : {
  "AvailabilityZone" : String,
  "CidrBlock" : String,
  "MapPublicIpOnLaunch" : Boolean,
  "Tags" : [ Resource Tag, ... ],
  "VpcId" : String
}
}
```

| Sno | Properties | Required | Type | Available values | Default value |
|---|---|---|---|---|---|
| 1 | AvailabilityZone | No | String | Example: "us-east-1a" | AWS automatically selects a zone |
| 2 | CIDRBlock | Yes | String | Example, 10.0.0.0/16 | NA |
| 3 | MapPublicIpOnLaunch | No | Boolean | True/False | FALSE |
| 4 | Tags | No | String | Key: String Value: String | NA |
| 5 | VpcId | Yes | Ref ID | Example: "Ref": vpc-12345678 | NA |

## Internet Gateway

The format for Internet Gateway is:

```
{
 "Type" : "AWS::EC2::InternetGateway",
"Properties" : {
   "Tags" : [ Resource Tag, ... ]
 }
 }
```

Example:

```
"InternetGateway" : {
   "Type" : "AWS::EC2::InternetGateway",
    "Properties" : {
   "Tags" : [ "Key" : "Name", "Value" : { "Ref" : "AWS::StackName"} ]
 }
   },
```

## Elastic IP

The format for Elastic IP is:

```
{
   "Type" : "AWS::EC2::EIP",
 "Properties" : {
    "InstanceId" : String,
"Domain" : String
  }
 }
```

| Sno | Properties | Required | Type |
|-----|-----------|----------|------|
| 1 | InstanceId | No | String |
| 2 | Domain | Conditional | String |

Example:

```
"EIP" : {
    "Type" : "AWS::EC2::EIP",
   "Properties" : {
      "Domain" : "vpc"
   }
 }
```

## Nat Gateway

The format for NAT Gateway is:

```
{
   "Type" : "AWS::EC2::NatGateway",
   "Properties" : {
     "AllocationId" : String,
     "SubnetId" : String
   }
}
```

| Sno | Properties | Required | Type |
|-----|-----------|----------|------|
| 1 | AllocationId | Yes | String |
| 2 | SubnetId | Yes | String |

Example:

```
"NATGateway" : {
    "Type" : "AWS::EC2::NatGateway",
    "DependsOn": "VPCGatewayAttach",
"Properties" : {
 "AllocationId" : { "Fn::GetAtt" : ["NATGatewayEIP", "AllocationId"]},
 "SubnetId" : { "Ref" : "PublicSubnet"}
 }
}
```

# Storing the template

- When you upload a template in CloudFormation to create your stack, CloudFormation will by default store the template into S3
- Upload the source code into S3 and maintain versions of the template
- It's good to store the template into source control

# Testing the JSON template

There are many tools available for JSON format testing, for example: `https://jsonlint.com/`.

```
 1 ▾ {
 2      "AWSTemplateFormatVersion": "2010-09-09",
 3      "Description": "Builds a VPC with Internet Gateway, 1 public and 1 private subnets and NAT Gateway.",
 4
 5 ▾    "Parameters": {
 6
 7 ▾        "VpcCidr": {
 8              "Description": "Enter the whole VPC CIDR Block.",
 9              "Type": "String",
10              "ConstraintDescription": "Supports subnet sizes of /16 to /22 only. Input must be a correct CIDR, such as: 10.0.0.0/16'
11              "AllowedPattern": "^((\\d)+.){3}(0)\\/(16|17|18|19|20|21|22)"
12          },
13
14 ▾        "PublicSubnetCIDR": {
```

Validate JSON    Clear                          Support JSONLint for $2/Month

**Results**

valid JSON

Testing JSON Template

# There's more...

There are a few best practices that you can follow while creating and storing your templates:

- Never embed credentials into the template; use input parameters to pass sensitive information to your environment.

- Be specific when providing access to any user to CloudFormation because modifying/deleting a CloudFormation stack can lead to unexpected disasters.
- Use the service role's policy to make calls instead of the user's policy.
- You can also store templates in a source repository such as GitHub or SVN and use the same template to replicate the environment in other regions.
- Make sure the resources you specify in the template don't hit the resource limit, otherwise your stack creation will fail.
- Always validate the template before using it. You can validate it by using CloudFormation or any other third-party tool.
- To modify the changes in the stack, always use change sets instead of direct updates. Using change sets will help in reviewing the changes. Both types of stack updates are mentioned in further recipes.

# Creating a new stack--CloudFormation

A Cloudformation stack acts as a single unit to provision and manage your stack. All the resources in the stack are defined in **Templates**. A stack can include all the resources for creating your multi-tier architecture or a single server, and whenever you don't need the server/infrastructure, you can instantly delete the stack. Deleting the stack will terminate and release all the resources associated with it.

## Getting ready

You will need to have the required permissions for VPC and CloudFormation. Also, keep your CIDR block ready for VPC and subnets. Be very careful when choosing your CIDR block, as you cannot update it later.

## How to do it...

The steps for creating a new stack on CloudFormation are as follows:

1. Log in to the AWS console.

Account: awsaccount

User Name: jhalak

Password: ●●●●●●●●●●●●●●

MFA users, enter your code on the next screen.

Sign In

Sign-in using root account credentials

Login into AWS console

2.  Go to **CloudFormation** service, as shown in the following screenshot:

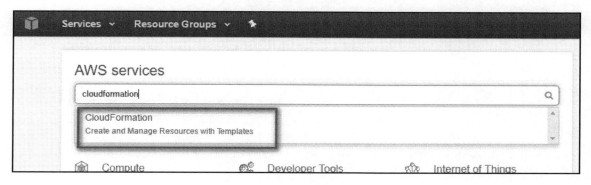

Search CloudFormation

3. Click on **Create New Stack**, as shown in the following screenshot:

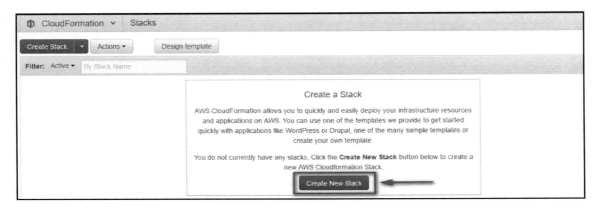

CloudFormation Console

4. The code for **Upload a template to Amazon S3** is available at `https://github.com/PacktPublishing/AWS-Networking-Cookbook`:

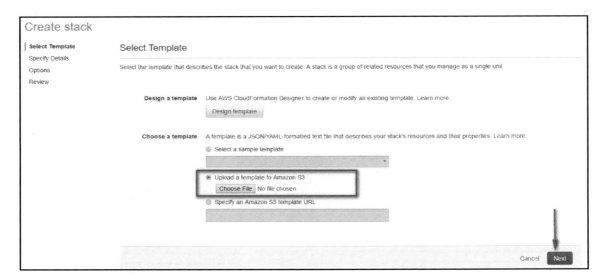

Select Template

5. Provide a CIDR for your VPC, private, and public subnet, then click on **Next**, as shown in the following screenshot:

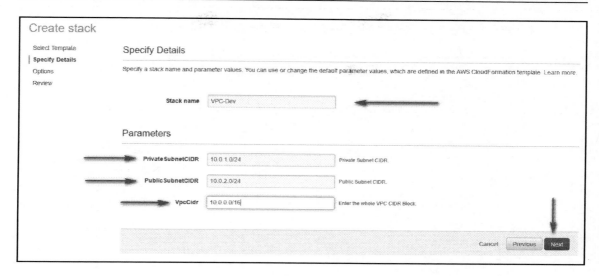

Provide Subnet Details

6. Provide the additional tag if required, then click **Next**.

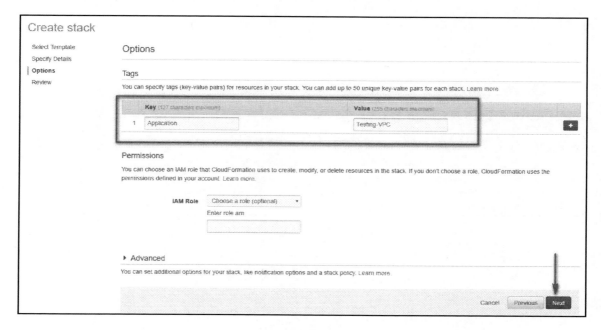

Provide Additional Tags

7. Review the stack and click **Create**, as shown in the following screenshot:

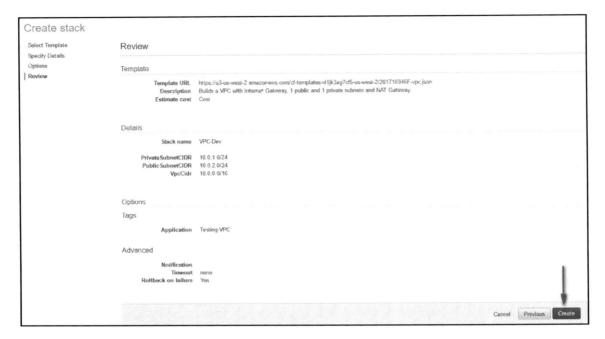

Review Stack Creation

8. You will get the following screen:

Stack Creation

9. Once all the resources have been created, the **Status** will be updated as **CREATE_COMPLETE**, as shown in the following screenshot:

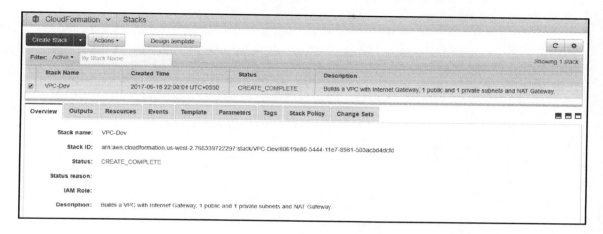

Stack Overview

10. You will get all the details of the created resources in the **Outputs** section.

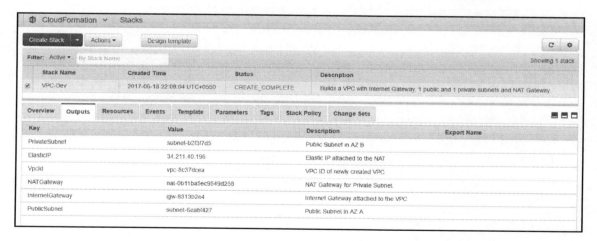

Stack Output

11. Now let's check the VPC (**AWS Dashboard | VPC | Select Your VPC**).

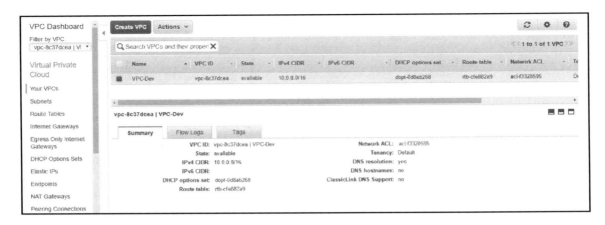

Stack: AWS VPC

12. Subnets (**AWS Dashboard | VPC | Subnets** provides a filter of your VPCs if you have multiple VPCs):

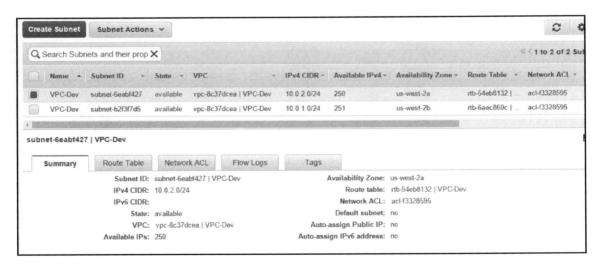

Stack: AWS VPC Subnets

13. Tags will look as shown in the following screenshot:

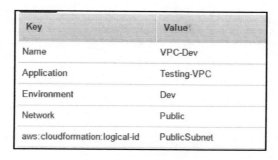

| Key | Value |
|---|---|
| Name | VPC-Dev |
| Application | Testing-VPC |
| Environment | Dev |
| Network | Public |
| aws:cloudformation:logical-id | PublicSubnet |

Stack: AWS VPC Subnet Tags

14. NAT Gateway (**AWS Dashboard** | **VPC** | **NAT Gateway** or use VPC filter to get the details).

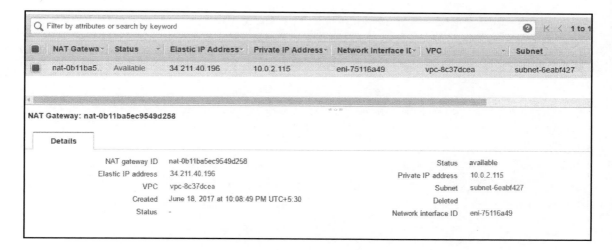

Stack: AWS VPC NAT Gateway

15. Internet Gateway (**AWS Dashboard** | **VPC** | **Internet Gateway**):

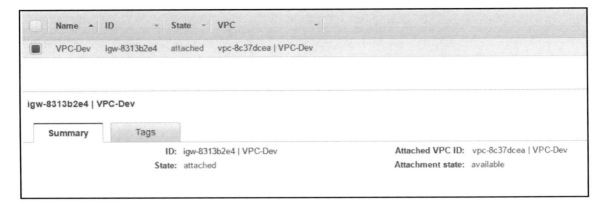

Stack: AWS VPC Internet Gateway

16. Route Table (**AWS Dashboard** | **VPC** | **Route Table**):

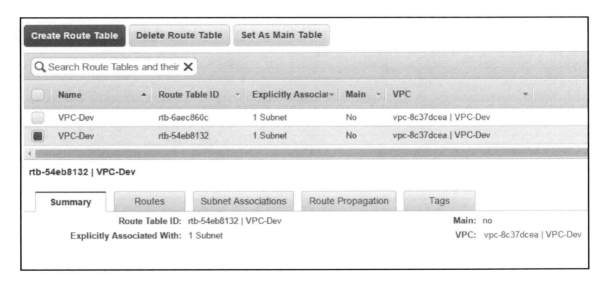

Stack: AWS VPC Route Table

17. Elastic IP (**AWS Dashboard | VPC | Elastic IP**):

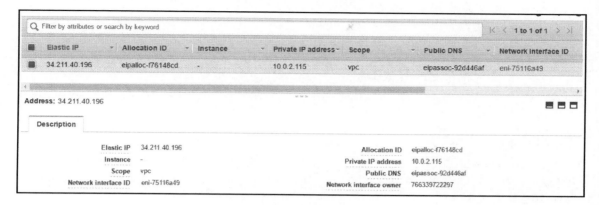

Stack: AWS VPC Elastic IP

18. VPC and all its components have been created successfully.

# How it works...

Templates define all the resources that need to be created, so when you create a stack, CloudFormation makes the underlying service calls to AWS to provision and configure your resources. CloudFormation resource creation does not depend on how you mention them in your template until you specify to create the resources one after another. You can use the DependsOn attribute to specify the creation of your resources.

# Modify the stack--CloudFormation

Now, we will modify/update the stack. For modifying, we will use the same template and add one more subnet into the VPC. CloudFormation provides two methods for modifying your stack:

1. **Direct update**:
   - When you submit the changes, CloudFormation deploys them immediately
   - You want to have a quick update on the stack
   - Works well when you are sure of the changes

2. **Change sets**:
   - Will allow you to preview the changes
   - Will not make the changes until you execute the change set
   - Provides a JSON formatted document to summarize the changes
   - Creates multiple change sets of different changes by providing a modified template

# Getting ready

Before going forward into this recipe, make sure you know how you want to update your changes. If you are sure with your changes, then select the direct update method, otherwise it is always preferred to use change sets (as we get time to review the changes).

# How to do it...

The following subsection will include how to make use of change sets and direct updates as a part of the CloudFormation update.

## Using change sets

The steps to create change sets are as follows:

1. In the CloudFormation console, select your stack.

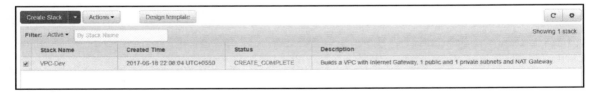

CloudFormation Stack

2. Select **Actions** | **Create Change Set For Current Stack**.

Modify Stack

3. Select **Upload a template to Amazon S3**, upload the updated template from `https://github.com/PacktPublishing/AWS-Networking-Cookbook` **and click Next**.

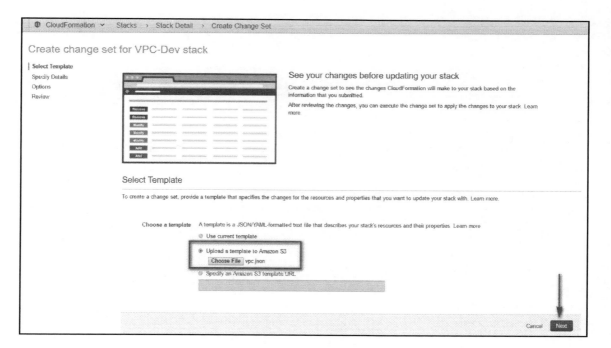

Upload the modified template

4. On the **Specify Details** page, current stack values will be available, as shown in the following screenshot:

Current VPC details

5. Provide **Change Set name**, brief **Description,** and **PublicSubnetCIDR2**. Then choose **Next.**

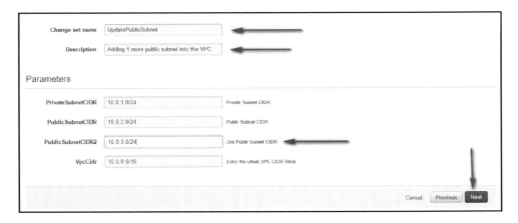

Provide modified VPC details

6. On the **Options** page, we can go for additional changes (such as stack's service role, stack tags, or Amazon SNS notification topic), and then click **Next**.

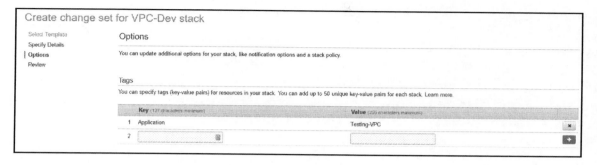

Provide Additional tags

7. Review the changes to the **Change Set** and click **Create Change Sets**.

Create change set for VPC-Dev stack

Select Template
Specify Details
Options
Review

Review

Template

Template URL    https://s3-us-west-2.amazonaws.com/cf-templates-vi1jk3ag7cf5-us-west-2/2017170tHRg-vpc.json
Description    Builds a VPC with Internet Gateway, 1 public and 1 private subnets and NAT Gateway

Details

Stack name    VPC-Dev

Change set name    UpdatePublicSubnet
Change set description    Adding 1 more public subnet into the VPC

PrivateSubnetCIDR    10.0.1.0/24
PublicSubnetCIDR    10.0.2.0/24
PublicSubnetCIDR2    10.0.3.0/24
VpcCidr    10.0.0.0/16

Options

Tags

Application    Testing-VPC

Advanced

Notification

Cancel    Previous    Create change set

Review and Create Change Set

8. Once the change set review has been completed, the Status will be **CREATE_COMPLETE**.

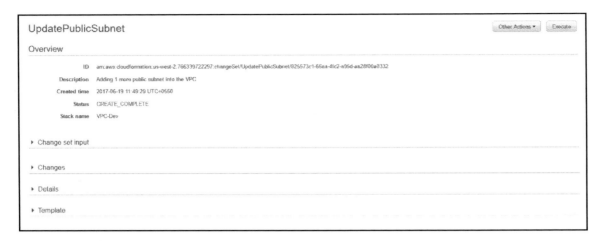

Change Set Status

9. The change set will be available at the CloudFormation console, select stack and **Change Sets**.

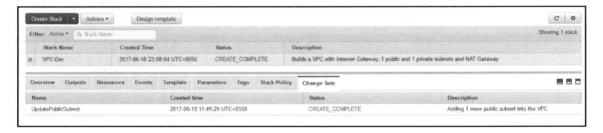

Change Sets Details

10. Let's check each section of the change set.

- **Changes**:

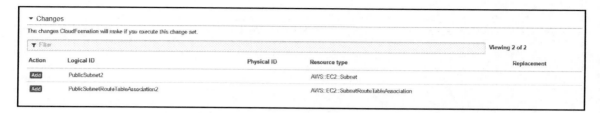

Change Set: Changes

- **Change Set input**:

### Change set input

The information that was submitted. CloudFormation used this information to generate this change set.

Tags

| Key | Value |
| --- | --- |
| Application | Testing-VPC |

Parameters

| Key | Value |
| --- | --- |
| PrivateSubnetCIDR | 10.0.1.0/24 |
| PublicSubnetCIDR | 10.0.2.0/24 |
| PublicSubnetCIDR2 | 10.0.3.0/24 |
| VpcCidr | 10.0.0.0/16 |

Amazon SNS topic ARN
No values submitted

Capabilities
No values submitted

Change Set: Change Set Input

- **Details**:

```
▼ Details
Detailed information about each change. For descriptions of each field, see the Change data type.

[
  {
    "resourceChange": {
      "logicalResourceId": "PublicSubnet2",
      "action": "Add",
      "physicalResourceId": null,
      "resourceType": "AWS::EC2::Subnet",
      "replacement": null,
      "details": [],
      "scope": []
    },
    "type": "Resource"
  },
  {
    "resourceChange": {
      "logicalResourceId": "PublicSubnetRouteTableAssociation2",
      "action": "Add",
      "physicalResourceId": null,
      "resourceType": "AWS::EC2::SubnetRouteTableAssociation",
      "replacement": null,
      "details": [],
      "scope": []
    },
    "type": "Resource"
  }
]
```

Change Set: Changes Details

- Template: Will show the entire updated template

11. Once all looks good, you can make the changes by executing the change set. (**Change set | Execute**).

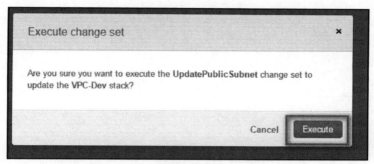

Update Stack

12. All the change sets have been deleted and the stack **Status** is **UPDATE_IN_PROGRESS**.

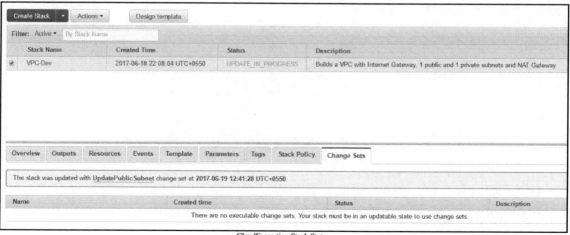

CloudFormation Stack Status

13. Now the Stack status is **UPDATE_COMPLETE** and the new subnet can be seen in the output section.

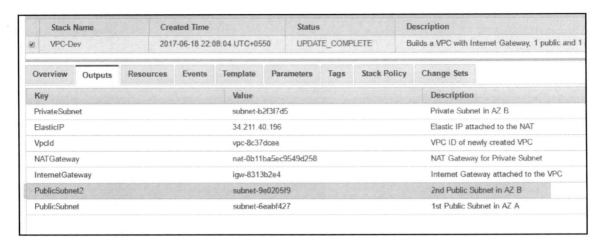

| Stack Name | Created Time | Status | Description |
|---|---|---|---|
| ☑ VPC-Dev | 2017-06-18 22:08:04 UTC+0550 | UPDATE_COMPLETE | Builds a VPC with Internet Gateway, 1 public and 1 |

Overview | **Outputs** | Resources | Events | Template | Parameters | Tags | Stack Policy | Change Sets

| Key | Value | Description |
|---|---|---|
| PrivateSubnet | subnet-b2f3f7d5 | Private Subnet in AZ B |
| ElasticIP | 34.211.40.196 | Elastic IP attached to the NAT |
| VpcId | vpc-8c37dcea | VPC ID of newly created VPC |
| NATGateway | nat-0b11ba5ec9549d258 | NAT Gateway for Private Subnet |
| InternetGateway | igw-8313b2e4 | Internet Gateway attached to the VPC |
| PublicSubnet2 | subnet-9e0205f9 | 2nd Public Subnet in AZ B |
| PublicSubnet | subnet-6eabf427 | 1st Public Subnet in AZ A |

CloudFormation Updated Output

# Using direct update

In this example, we will be adding a private subnet in the VPC.

1. Log in to the CloudFormation console and select the stack that you want to update.
2. Choose **Action** | **Update stack**.

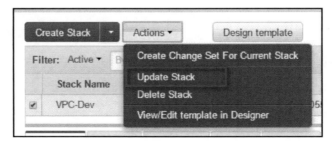

CloudFormation Stack Direct Update

3. Provide the updated file and click **Next**. The file is available at `https://github.com/PacktPublishing/AWS-Networking-Cookbook`.

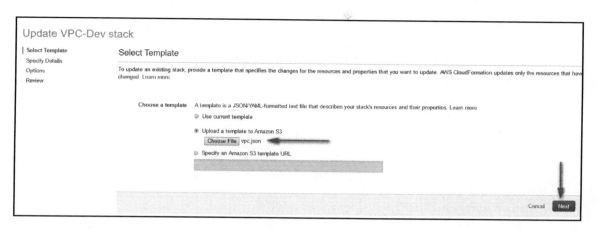

Upload template to update Stack

4. Provide the **Private SubnetCIDR** : `10.0.4.0/24`.

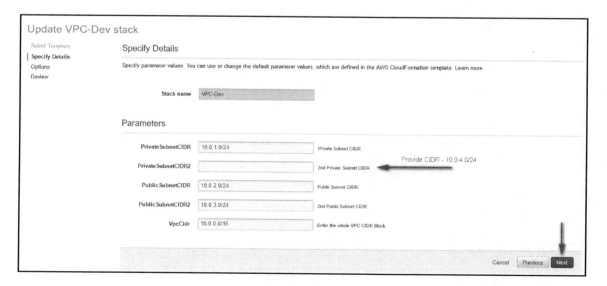

Provide Updated Subnet Details

5. In the **Options** tab, add or update tags if required, otherwise click **Next**.
6. Review the changes.

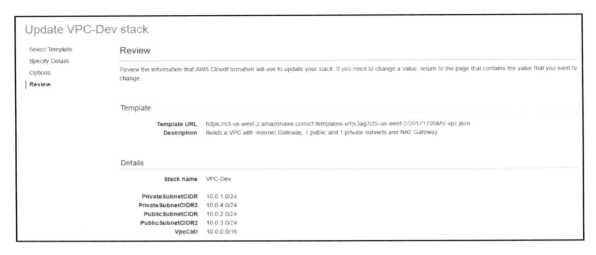

Review Updation

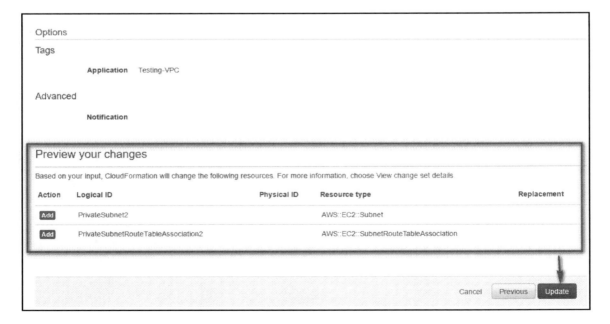

CloudFormation Update Stack

7. The updated process can be seen in the **Events** section.

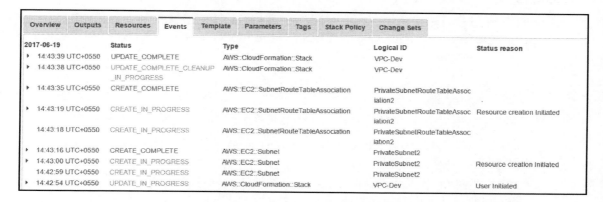

CloudFormation Stack updation in process

8. The **Outputs** section will give the details of created resources. For example, Subnet ID.

CloudFormation Updated Output

# Deleting the stack--CloudFormation

Think twice before performing this step, as deleting the stack will delete all the resources associated with it. You can delete a stack by using the AWS console or CLI.

## Getting ready

Follow the steps to delete the stack. The following are a few points to remember:

1. After stack deletion has begun, you cannot stop it. The stack proceeds to the **DELETE_IN_PROGRESS** state.
2. Stack deletion will delete all the resources associated with it.
3. By default, deleted stacks will not be visible in CloudFormation. To view the deleted stacks, change the filter to **Deleted**.
4. Templates of deleted stacks will be available in S3 as well.

## How to do it...

The steps to delete a CloudFormation stack:

1. Log in to the CloudFormation console and select the stack.

CloudFormation Stack

2. Click **Actions | Delete stack**.

3. Click **Yes, Delete** when prompted.

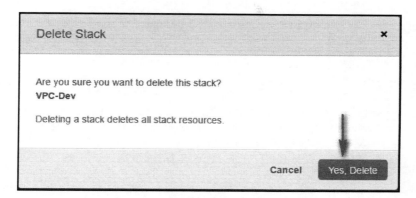

Delete CloudFormation Stack

4. Stack status will change to **DELETE_IN_PROGRESS**.

CloudFormation Stack Delete Status

5. Stacks can be viewed by changing the filter to **Deleted**.

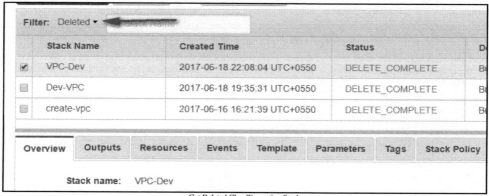

Get Deleted CloudFormation Stack

# There's more...

Use the following command to delete the stack using CLI:

```
# aws cloudformation delete-stack --stack-name VPC-Dev
```

# Setting up Ansible

Ansible is an automation tool for the configuration, provisioning, and management of cloud and on-prem resources. It makes a difference in the way of deployment as it is an SSH-based tool and comes with a very easy and secure connection. It is very easy to get started with Ansible for people coming from a Linux background.

Ansible is an agentless tool, you need to install it in on one controller machine and whenever you want to make a deployment, run it from your controller machine, provide the host list, and deploy it in all the nodes. All commands are run through Ansible via SSH, and if Ansible needs updating, you only need to update your single control machine.

You can also check the version and software status, for example, if you want to check whether Apache is installed on all the machines or not, Ansible will give you a machine list where Apache is not installed and will allow you to install it on those machines keeping the other machines untouched.

# Getting ready

Playbooks are written in `.yaml` and tend to follow a process with minimum syntax. Each playbook can have one or more plays on the list. An Ansible playbook is the simplest way to achieve configuration management, orchestration, and multimachine deployment.

# How to do it...

Let's look at VPC and other resource creation snippets:

1. VPC creation example:

```
- ec2_vpc:
    state: present
    cidr_block: 10.0.0.0/16
    resource_tags: { "Environment":"Development" }
  region: us-west-2
```

2. Subnet creation example:

```
subnets:
         - cidr: 172.22.1.0/24
           az: us-west-2c
           resource_tags: { "Environment":"Dev", "Tier" : "Web" }
```

3. Internet Gateway:

```
internet_gateway: True
        route_tables:
          - subnets:
              - 172.22.2.0/24
              - 172.22.3.0/24
            routes:
              - dest: 0.0.0.0/0
                gw: igw
```

4. Creating a NAT Gateway:

```
- name: Create new nat gateway and allocate new EIP.
  ec2_vpc_nat_gateway:
    state: present
    subnet_id: subnet-12345678
    wait: yes
    region: ap-southeast-2
  register: new_nat_gateway
```

5. Deleting a VPC:

```
- ec2_vpc:
   state: absent
   vpc_id: vpc-aaaaaaa
    region: us-west-2
```

# Installing Ansible

There are several ways to install Ansible. We will be cloning the full repository from Git and then installing it. The following are the steps:

1. Log in to the EC2 console (the steps have already been provided in Chapter 2, *Building Your Own Custom VPC*, in recipe, *Managing EC2 instances*).

2.  Launch an EC2 server (the steps have already been provided in Chapter 2, *Building Your Own Custom VPC*, in recipe, *Managing EC2 instances*).

EC2 Server

3.  Log in to the server.

EC2 Linux Server Login

4.  Install Ansible (RHEL/Ubuntu).
5.  Change the hostname.

```
[root@ip-172-31-18-87 ~] # hostname ansible
```

6. Check whether Python is installed with 2.x version (because a version below 2.x is not compatible with Ansible).

```
[root@ansible ~]# python -V
Python 2.7.12
```

7. Enable the EPEL repository on Amazon Linux. Go to your yum.repos.d folder and enable epel.repo (modify enabled=0 to enabled=1).

```
[root@ansible ansible]# vim /etc/yum.repos.d/epel.repo
```

Enable EPEL Repo

8. Type – esc :wq.

9. Follow the following steps to install Ansible:

```
[root@ansible ~ ]# yum install ansible
Loaded plugins: priorities, update-motd, upgrade-helper
...
```

```
Installed:  ansible.noarch 0:2.3.1.0-1.el6
Dependency Installed:
python-crypto2.6.x86_64 0:2.6.1-2.el6                    python-
jinja2-26.noarch 0:2.6-3.el6
python-keyczar.noarch 0:0.71c-1.el6                     python26.x86_64
0:2.6.9-2.88.amzn1
python26-PyYAML.x86_64 0:3.10-3.10.amzn1                python26-
babel.noarch 0:0.9.4-5.1.8.amzn1
python26-backports.x86_64 0:1.0-3.14.amzn1             python26-
backports-ssl_match_hostname.noarch 0:3.4.0.2-1.12.amzn1
python26-crypto.x86_64 0:2.6.1-1.14.amzn1              python26-
ecdsa.noarch 0:0.11-3.3.amzn1
python26-httplib2.noarch 0:0.7.7-1.5.amzn1             python26-
libs.x86_64 0:2.6.9-2.88.amzn1
python26-markupsafe.x86_64 0:0.11-4.6.amzn1            python26-
paramiko.noarch 0:1.15.1-1.5.amzn1
python26-pyasn1.noarch 0:0.1.7-2.9.amzn1               python26-
setuptools.noarch 0:12.2-1.32.amzn1
python26-simplejson.x86_64 0:3.6.5-1.12.amzn1          python26-
six.noarch 0:1.8.0-1.23.amzn1
sshpass.x86_64 0:1.06-1.el6
Complete!
```

10. Follow these steps if you want to install the latest version of Ansible (Ansible 2.4.1.0):

```
[root@ansible ~ ]# yum install git -y
[root@ansible ~ ]# mkdir ansibletmp
 [root@ansible ~ ]# cd ./ansibletmp
 [root@ansible ansibletmp ]# git clone
git://github.com/ansible/ansible.git -recursive
 Cloning into '-recursive'...
 remote: Counting objects: 267737, done.
 remote: Compressing objects: 100% (28/28), done.
 remote: Total 267737 (delta 11), reused 1 (delta 0), pack-reused
267709
 Receiving objects: 100% (267737/267737), 76.53 MiB | 13.51 MiB/s,
done.
 Resolving deltas: 100% (170624/170624), done.
 Checking connectivity... done.
 [root@ansible ansibletmp ]# cd ./ansible
 [root@ansible ansible]# source ./hacking/env-setup
 [root@ansible ansible]# ansible --version
 ansible 2.4.0
 config file = None
 configured module search path =
[u'/root/.ansible/plugins/modules',
u'/usr/share/ansible/plugins/modules']
```

```
ansible python module location = /usr/local/lib/python2.7/site-
packages/ansible-2.4.0-py2.7.egg/ansible
 executable location = /root/ansible/bin/ansible
 python version = 2.7.12 (default, Sep 1 2016, 22:14:00) [GCC 4.8.3
20140911 (Red Hat 4.8.3-9)]
```

11. You can set up the host file for adding different hosts, but here we will be creating a VPC so we can skip the host entry.

12. As we are using Amazon AMI, AWS CLI is already installed, otherwise it can be installed using the following commands:

```
[root@ansible ansible]# yum install python-pipOr
[root@ansible ansible]# curl -O
https://bootstrap.pypa.io/get-pip.py
[root@ansible ansible]# python get-pip.py
[root@ansible ansible]# pip install awscli
[root@ansible ansible]# aws --version
[root@ansible ansible]# aws configure
```

13. Ansible has been installed successfully.

# Creating Ansible playbooks for creating VPC

We will be creating Ansible playbooks for managing VPC.

## How to do it...

The following are the steps for creating Ansible playbooks:

1. Create a new playbook. The folder structure will be as follows:

```
[root@ansible ~ ]# cd /etc/ansible/
[root@ansible ansible]# mkdir playbook
[root@ansible ansible]# mkdir playbook/roles
[root@ansible ansible]# mkdir playbook/roles/vpc
[root@ansible ansible]# mkdir playbook/roles/vpc/{defaults,tasks}
[root@ansible ansible]# cd playbook
```

2. Create the configuration file in the `playbook` folder `awsvpc.yml`.

```
[root@ansible playbook]# vim awsvpc.yml
---
- name: Create VPC
 hosts: localhost
 gather_facts: no
 roles:
 - vpc
```

1. Create a file `inventory` in `playbook` folder and can be found at `https://github.com/PacktPublishing/AWS-Networking-Cookbook`.

```
[root@ansible playbook]# vim inventory
[local]
localhost ansible_connection=local
```

2. Create a file `main.yml` in `playbook/roles/vpc/tasks/` folder. This file will contain the configurations required for your VPC and can be found at `https://github.com/PacktPublishing/AWS-Networking-Cookbook`.

```
[root@ansible playbook]# vim roles/vpc/tasks/main.yml
---
- name: Create VPC inside mention region
 ec2_vpc:
 state: present
 cidr_block: "{{ vpc_cidr_block }}"
 region: "{{ vpc_region }}"
 resource_tags: { "Name":"{{ vpc_name }}-vpc" }
 subnets:
 - cidr: "{{ public_cidr_1 }}" # Private Subnet 1
 az: "{{ vpc_region }}a"
 resource_tags: { "Name":"{{ vpc_name }}-private-subnet" }
 - cidr: "{{ public_cidr_2 }}" # Public Subnet 2
 az: "{{ public_az_2 }}"
 resource_tags: { "Name":"{{ vpc_name }}-{{ public_az_2 }}-
public-subnet" }
 internet_gateway: yes
 route_tables:
 - subnets:
 - "{{ public_cidr_2 }}"
 routes:
 - dest: 0.0.0.0/0
 gw: igw
 register: vpc
```

3. Create a file `main.yml` in `playbook/roles/vpc/defaults/` folder and can be found at `https://github.com/PacktPublishing/AWS-Networking-Cookbook`. This file will contain the VPC details required for your VPC. For example: VPC name, region, and so on.

```
[root@ansible playbook]# vim roles/vpc/defaults/main.yml
---
vpc_name: dev-vpc
vpc_region: us-west-2 # Oregon
vpc_cidr_block: 10.0.0.0/16
public_cidr_1: 10.0.10.0/24
public_az_1: "{{ vpc_region }}a"
public_cidr_2: 10.0.20.0/24
public_az_2: "{{ vpc_region }}b"
```

4. Run the `playbook` by providing following commands:

```
[root@ansible playbook]# ansible-playbook -i inventory
awsvpc.yml
 PLAY [Create VPC]
***********************************************************
***********************************************************
******************************
 TASK [vpc : Create VPC inside mention region]
***********************************************************
***********************************************************
****
 changed: [localhost]
 PLAY RECAP
***********************************************************
***********************************************************
*****************************************
 localhost : ok=1 changed=1 unreachable=0 failed=0
 # If you get any error try checking in verbose by adding -
vvv in the end
 [root@ip-172-31-12-123 playbook]# ansible-playbook -i
inventory awsvpc.yml -vvv
 Using /etc/ansible/ansible.cfg as config file
 PLAYBOOK: awsvpc.yml
***********************************************************
***********************************************************
**************************
 1 plays in awsvpc.yml
 PLAY [Create VPC]
***********************************************************
***********************************************************
******************************
```

```
META: ran handlers
TASK [vpc : Create VPC inside mention region]
*************************************************************
*************************************************************
****
task path:
/etc/ansible/playbook/roles/vpc/tasks/main.yml:3
 Using module file /usr/lib/python2.6/site-
packages/ansible/modules/cloud/amazon/_ec2_vpc.py
 <localhost> ESTABLISH LOCAL CONNECTION FOR USER: root
 <localhost> EXEC /bin/sh -c 'echo ~ && sleep 0'
 <localhost> EXEC /bin/sh -c '( umask 77 && mkdir -p "`
echo /root/.ansible/tmp/ansible-
tmp-1498048548.85-61490596099452 `" && echo ansible-
tmp-1498048548.85-61490596099452="` echo
/root/.ansible/tmp/ansible-tmp-1498048548.85-61490596099452
`" ) && sleep 0'
 <localhost> PUT /tmp/tmpeDeueO TO
/root/.ansible/tmp/ansible-
tmp-1498048548.85-61490596099452/_ec2_vpc.py
 <localhost> EXEC /bin/sh -c 'chmod u+x
/root/.ansible/tmp/ansible-
tmp-1498048548.85-61490596099452/
/root/.ansible/tmp/ansible-
tmp-1498048548.85-61490596099452/_ec2_vpc.py && sleep 0'
 <localhost> EXEC /bin/sh -c '/usr/bin/python
/root/.ansible/tmp/ansible-
tmp-1498048548.85-61490596099452/_ec2_vpc.py; rm -rf
"/root/.ansible/tmp/ansible-
tmp-1498048548.85-61490596099452/" > /dev/null 2>&1 &&
sleep 0'
 ok: [localhost] => {
 "changed": false,
 "igw_id": "igw-993d9ffe",
 "invocation": {
 "module_args": {
 "aws_access_key": null,
 "aws_secret_key": null,
 "cidr_block": "10.0.0.0/16",
 "dns_hostnames": true,
 "dns_support": true,
 "ec2_url": null,
 "instance_tenancy": "default",
 "internet_gateway": true,
 "profile": null,
 "region": "us-west-2",
 "resource_tags": {
 "Name": "dev-vpc-vpc"
```

```
},
"route_tables": [
{
"routes": [
{
"dest": "0.0.0.0/0",
"gw": "igw"
}
],
"subnets": [
"10.0.20.0/24"
]
}
],
"security_token": null,
"state": "present",
"subnets": [
{
"az": "us-west-2a",
"cidr": "10.0.10.0/24",
"resource_tags": {
"Name": "dev-vpc-private-subnet"
}
},
{
"az": "us-west-2b",
"cidr": "10.0.20.0/24",
"resource_tags": {
"Name": "dev-vpc-us-west-2b-public-subnet"
}
}
],
"validate_certs": true,
"vpc_id": null,
"wait": false,
"wait_timeout": "300"
}
},
"subnets": [
{
"az": "us-west-2a",
"cidr": "10.0.10.0/24",
"id": "subnet-11edb558",
"resource_tags": {
"Name": "dev-vpc-private-subnet"
}
},
{
```

```
"az": "us-west-2b",
"cidr": "10.0.20.0/24",
"id": "subnet-efb2b388",
"resource_tags": {
"Name": "dev-vpc-us-west-2b-public-subnet"
}
}
],
"vpc": {
"cidr_block": "10.0.0.0/16",
"dhcp_options_id": "dopt-0d8ab268",
"id": "vpc-b647b3d0",
"region": "us-west-2",
"state": "available"
},
"vpc_id": "vpc-b647b3d0"
}
META: ran handlers
META: ran handlers
PLAY RECAP
*********************************************************
*********************************************************
************************************************
localhost : ok=1 changed=0 unreachable=0 failed=0
[root@ip-172-31-12-123 playbook]#
```

3. VPC and subnets are now available in the AWS console:

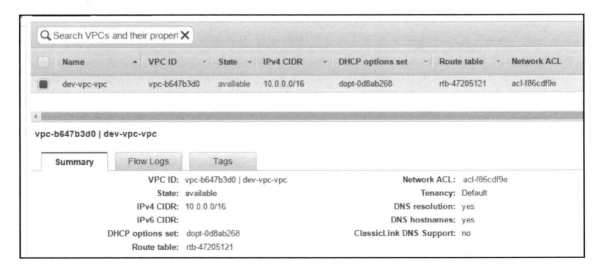

Ansible: VPC

4. Private subnet without IGW.

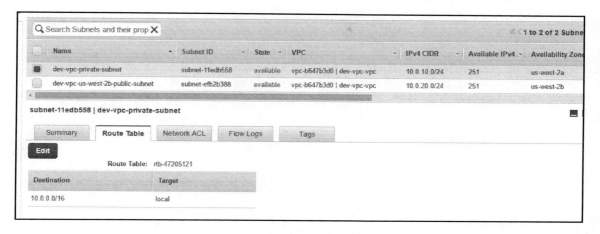

Ansible: VPC Subnet

5. Public subnet with IGW.

Ansible: Public Subnet Route Table

# There's more...

The following are a few sample playbooks for various VPC configurations. You can use the following playbooks by replacing `main.yml` in (`/etc/ansible/playbook/roles/tasks/main.yml`).

Use the following code to create a VPC with a single public subnet (`https://github.com/PacktPublishing/AWS-Networking-Cookbook`):

```
---
- name: Create VPC inside mention region
  ec2_vpc:
    state: present
    cidr_block: "{{ vpc_cidr_block }}"
    region: "{{ vpc_region }}"
    resource_tags: { "Name":"{{ vpc_name }}-vpc" }
    subnets:
   - cidr: "{{ public_cidr_1 }}" # Public Subnet-1
    az: "{{ public_az_1 }}"
    resource_tags: { "Name":"{{ vpc_name }}-{{ public_az_1 }}-public-
subnet" }
    internet_gateway: yes
    route_tables: "{{ public_subnet_rt }}"
    - subnets:
      - "{{ public_cidr_1 }}"
        routes:
      - dest: 0.0.0.0/0
        gw: igw
        register: vpc
```

Use following code to create VPC with private subnet and NAT Gateway (`https://github.com/PacktPublishing/AWS-Networking-Cookbook`):

```
---
- name: Create VPC inside mention region
  ec2_vpc:
    state: present
    cidr_block: "{{ vpc_cidr_block }}"
    region: "{{ vpc_region }}"
    resource_tags: { "Name":"{{ vpc_name }}-vpc" }
    internet_gateway: yes
  register: new_vpc
- name: Create private subnet
  ec2_vpc_subnet:    state: present
    vpc_id: "{{ new_vpc.vpc_id }}"
    az: "{{ public_az_1 }}"
    cidr: "{{ public_cidr_1 }}" # Private Subnet-1
```

```
      region: "{{ vpc_region }}"
      resource_tags: { "Name":"{{ vpc_name }}-{{ public_az_1 }}-private-
subnet" }
     vpc_id: "{{ new_vpc.vpc_id }}"
    register: private_subnet
  - name: Create new nat gateway using an EIP address
    ec2_vpc_nat_gateway:
      state: present
      subnet_id: "{{ private_subnet.subnet.id }}"
      wait: yes
      region: "{{ vpc_region }}"
      if_exist_do_not_create: true
    register: vpc_nat_gateway
  - name: Modify private subnet
    ec2_vpc_route_table:
      vpc_id: '{{ new_vpc.vpc_id }}'
      region: '{{ vpc_region }}'
      subnets: "{{ private_subnet.subnet.id }}"
      routes:
        - dest: 0.0.0.0/0
          gateway_id: "{{ vpc_nat_gateway.nat_gateway_id }}"
```

# 6
# Working with Route 53

In this chapter, we will cover the following recipes:

- Registering a new domain
- Transferring a domain into Amazon Route 53
- Creating hosted zones and record sets
- Deleting a public hosted zone
- Creating an Alias record set
- Creating a private hosted zone
- Working with the weighted routing policy
- Working with the failover routing policy and health checks

## Introduction

Route 53 is a highly available and scalable domain name service and primarily provides the following four functionalities:

- Domain management: Allows you to register a new domain and transfers the existing domain
- DNS management:
  - Route 53 translates friendly domain names such as `abc.com` into IP addresses such as `1.2.3.4`.
  - Route 53 uses its authoritative DNS server across a global network to respond to DNS queries, which helps in reducing latency.
  - Route 53 can route internet traffic to CloudFront distribution, Elastic Beanstalk endpoint, ELB record, or S3 bucket. Also, there's no extra charge for DNS queries to these resources.

- Traffic management
- Health check of the domain:
    - Route 53 monitors the health of your resources, such as web and email servers
    - Route 53 health checkers are placed globally
    - Route 53 automatically sends a request over the internet to the application to verify that it's reachable, available, and functional
    - You can also configure CloudWatch alarms to send a notification when a resource becomes unavailable
    - Route 53's failover policy helps in reconfiguring internet traffic away from resources that are unavailable or have failed health checks

# How does Route 53 DNS works?

The domain name system provides a mapping between human-readable names such as `www.abc.com` and the IP of their associated servers.

When you type an address in your browser `www.abc.com`:

- The operating system will first check the DNS in its local cache.
- Then it will look for the DNS in your LAN.
- Then the query will be forwarded to your DNS cache server (generally your ISP).

 These DNS cache servers are called *not authoritative DNS servers.*

- The request is then forwarded to the authoritative root name server responsible for maintaining a list of name servers for each of the top-level domains (.com, .org, and so on).
- Based on TLD, the request goes to the authoritative top-level domain name server responsible for maintaining a list of name servers for all domains (`www.gmail.com`, `www.wikipedia.org`, and so on). Its job is to query name servers to find and return the authoritative name server for the requested domain.

# Supported DNS resource record types

- **Address (A) record**
  - IPv4 address
  - <Value>192.0.2.1</Value>

- **AAAA** record
  - IPv6 address
  - <Value>2001:0db8:85a3:0:0:8a2e:0370:7334</Value>

- **CNAME** record
  - Canonical/Alternative Domain Name
  - <Value>hostname.example.com</Value>

- **Mail Xchange (MX)** record
  - Domain name of a mail host
  - <Value>10 mail.example.com</Value>

- **Name Server (NS)** record
  - Name Servers Record
  - <Value>ns-1.example.com</Value>

- **PTR** record
  - <Value>hostname.example.com</Value>

- **Start of Authority (SOA)** record:
  - Information stored in the DNS zone about that zone and about other DNS records
  - 7 fields: Primary authority, Contact detail, zone serial number, refresh time, retry time, expire time, and minimum time to live (TTL)
  - <Value>ns-2048.awsdns-64.net hostmaster.awsdns.com 1 1 1 1 60</Value>

- **Sender Policy Framework (SPF)** record
  - Used for verifying the identity of sender email messages
  - We recommend creating a TXT record instead of SPF
  - <Value>"v=spf1 ip4:192.168.0.1/16 -all"</Value>

- **SRV** record
  - Service record
  - 4 values: priority, weight, port, and domain name
  - <Value>10 5 80 hostname.example.com</Value>
- **TXT** record
  - It contains a space-separated list of double-quoted strings

# Alias resource record

- Route 53 supports alias records that give the flexibility to point our custom endpoints to the resource record set and TLD (abc.com)
- You can create alias record for CloudFront distribution, Elastic Beanstalk endpoint, ELB Endpoint, S3 bucket, or any other Route 53 resource record set
- You can use Alias record to point an apex zone (root domain without www, for example: google.com) to any custom DNS name
- As ELB and other resources change their IP frequently, Route 53 Alias makes this task easier by reflecting those changes automatically without making any changes to the hosted zone
- If an Alias resource record set points to a CloudFront distribution, a load balancer, or an S3 bucket, the **time to live (TTL)** can't be set; Route 53 uses the CloudFront, load balancer, or Amazon S3 TTLs

# Routing policies

Route 53 supports the below routing policies:

- **Simple routing policy**:
  - When you have a single resource for your domain to route your traffic
  - Example: IP address in an A record
- **Weighted routing policy**:
  - When you have multiple resources to perform the same role
  - For example: Route traffic to different resources in specified balances (weights) for example, 30% to one server and the remaining 40% to the other resource

- These resources can be a part of the same hosting group and can be on-premise as well
- You can also set up an active-active routing policy by setting up 50% weight to both the resources
- **Latency-based Routing (LBR) policy:**
    - Route 53 routes traffic, based on which the data center gives the user the lowest network latency
- **Failover routing policy:**
    - Route 53 allows an active-passive failover setup, where the primary resource responds to all traffic while keeping the secondary resource idle
    - If the primary resource becomes unavailable, the other resource takes all the traffic
- **Geolocation routing policy:**
    - Route 53 uses a geo-IP database and responds to DNS queries based on the user's geographic location

# Registering a new domain

You can find the available domains and registers using Route 53. It also supports registering an existing domain that you registered with other registrars. This recipe will explain how to register a new domain.

# Getting ready

You will need access to the Route 53 service and will need the below details as a part of the domain registration:

- Access to the email ID for domain confirmation
- Keep your domain name ready

# How to do it...

1. Log in to the AWS console and select **Route 53**.
2. Navigate to domain registration and click on **Get started now**.

Domain Registration: Get Started

3. Click on **Register Domain**.

Register domain

4. Type the domain name that you want to register and click **Check** to find out whether the domain name is available. This will give you multiple similar options in **Related Domain Suggestions**.

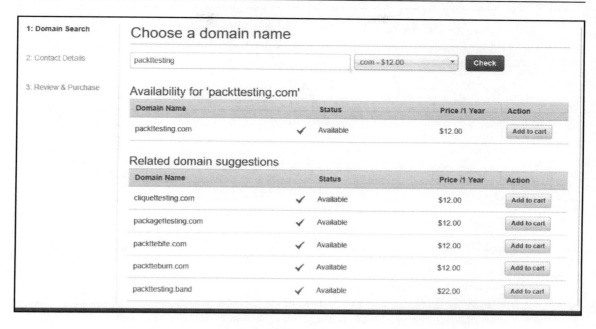

Choose domain name

5. Select the desired domain, click **Add to Cart**, and click **Continue** at the bottom of the page.

6. Provide your contact details, as asked, and click **Continue**.

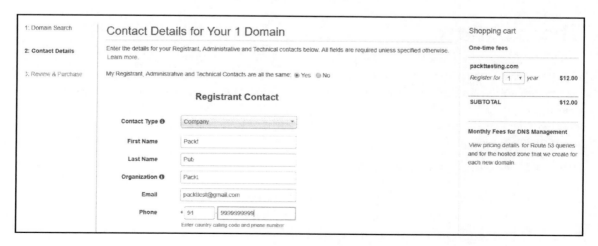

Provide contact details

7. Review the information you entered and read the terms of service. Select **I have read and agree to the AWS Domain Name Registration Agreement**, then click **Complete Purchase**.

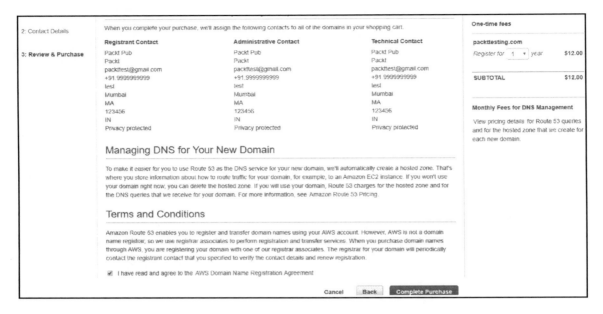

Review and complete domain registration

# There's more...

Once the domain registration is complete, the next step is to create a DNS, but when you register a domain from AWS Route 53, it registers a hosted zone automatically. A DNS can be created in Route 53 or you can use other providers. The usual renewal period of a domain is 1 year, some TLD (Top Level Domains) provide longer subscriptions as well. Wisely select the domain expiry. The period during which you can renew a domain varies from different TLDs.

The values that Route 53 returns after registration are as follows:

- **Registered on**: The date on which the domain is registered
- **Expires on**: The date and time (in GMT) when the domain is going to expire
- **Domain name status code**: Current status of the domain (Example: Registering, transferring, or renewing a domain)

- **Transfer Lock**: Enabled or Disabled (Enable the lock to reduce the possibility of transferring your domain to other registrars)
- **Auto renew**: Route 53 to automatically renew your domain or not
- **Authorization code**: This code is required for transferring the domain to any other registrar
- **Name servers**: List of name servers that are going to respond to the DNS queries for the domain.

# Transferring a domain into Amazon Route 53

You can transfer a domain from your current registrar to Amazon 53, or from one AWS account to another, or from Route 53 to another registrar. This recipe will explain how to transfer a domain and DNS to Route 53.

## Getting ready

There are a few minimum requirements:

- The domain registration or restoration with the previous registrar must be done at least 60 days before
- You cannot initiate a domain transfer if the current domain status is one of the following:
    - pendingDelete
    - pendingTransfer
    - redemptionPeriod
    - clientTransferProhibited
- Check whether Route 53 supports the TLD

# How to do it...

1. Confirm that Route 53 supports the TLD; you can get a list of the supported TLD's here: `http://docs.aws.amazon.com/Route53/latest/DeveloperGuide/registrar-tld-list.html`.

2. Transfer the DNS:
   1. Create a Route 53 hosted zone to get the name server details.
   2. Create all the resource record sets in a newly created hosted zone.

3. Change the settings with your current registrar (this process can differ with different registrars).
   1. Unlock the domain.
   2. Disable privacy protection from the domain.
   3. Get an authorization code.
   4. Disable DNSSEC for the domain.
   5. Check your contact information with the current registrar.

4. Request the transfer:
   1. Log in to the AWS console and select **Route 53**.
   2. Navigate to domain registration and click on **Get started now**.
   3. Choose **Transfer Domain**.
   4. Enter the name of the domain for which you want to transfer the registration to Amazon Route 53 and choose **Check**.
   5. If the domain registration is available for transfer, click **Add to Cart**. If the domain is not available, you will get a list of possible reasons.
   6. When you've added all the domain registrations that you want to transfer, choose **Continue**.
   7. Provide the following details:
      1. Authorization code.
      2. Name server options:
         1. Continue to use the name servers provided by the current registrar or DNS service.
         2. Import name servers from a Route 53 hosted zone that has the same name as the domain.
         3. Specify the new name servers to replace the current registrar's name servers (not recommended).
      3. Nameservers.

4. Glue records.

8. Provide your contact details as asked and click **Continue**.

9. Review the information you entered, read the terms of service, and select the checkbox to confirm that you've read the terms of service.

10. Choose **Complete Purchase**.

5. You will get a confirmation email on your registered email ID to continue the transfer (if the registrant contact authorizes the transfer, AWS starts to work with your current registrar to transfer your domain).

6. Update your domain configuration by changing the following details: (optional)
   - Transfer lock
   - Automatic renewal
   - Extended registration period
   - **Domain Name System Security Extensions (DNSSEC)**

# Creating hosted zones and record sets

Hosted zones store the information about how you want to route the traffic in the form of resource record sets. Records determine how DNS responds to your domain or subdomain. This recipe will explain how to create a hosted zone and resource record sets.

## Getting ready

Before creating hosted zones, make sure you have access to the domain name and the resources you are going to point to.

# How to do it...

1. Sign in to AWS console and click on **Route 53**.
2. In the **DNS management** section, click **Get started now**.

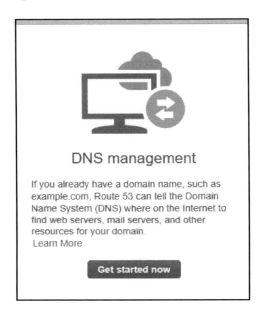

DNS: Get Started

3. Click **Create Hosted Zone**.

Hosted Zones

4. In the **Create Hosted Zone** pane, enter a **Domain Name** and optionally, a **Comment**.

5.  Select **Type** as **Public Hosted Zone** and click **Create**.

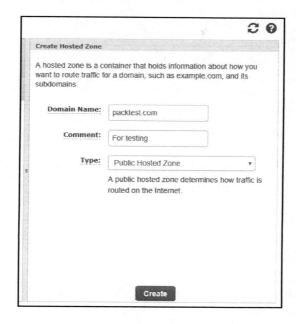

Hosted zone creation

6.  Once the hosted zones are created, it will by default create NS (Name Server) and SOA (Start of Authority) records.

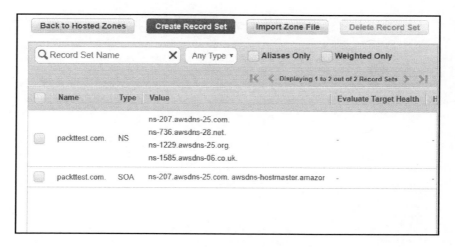

Hosted zone details

7. Click on **Create Record Set** to create a new record.
8. Provide the following values:
    1. **Name**: We will keep it blank, as we want to resolve `packttest.com` to an IP.
    2. Type: Select **A - IPv4 address**.

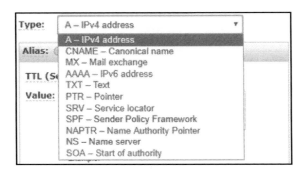

DNS: Select record type

    3. **Alias**: Select **No**.
    4. **TTL (Seconds)**: Default value of **300** seconds (five minutes).
    5. **Value**: Elastic IP address for your Amazon EC2 instance or provide the IP address of your web server.
    6. **Routing Policy**: Select **Simple**. Accept the default value of **Simple**.

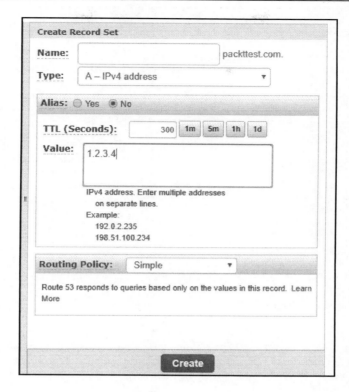

Create Resource Record Set

7. Click **Create**.

9. You can follow the same process to create `www.packttest.com`.

10. Test the URL by entering it in the browser.

# Deleting a public hosted zone

The following procedure explains how to delete a hosted zone using the Amazon Route 53 console.

# Getting ready

Deleting a hosted zone will destroy the current routing, hence take a backup before making any changes. Also, you can delete the hosted zone if there are no resource record sets associated with it, that is, before deleting the hosted zone we need to delete the records.

# How to do it...

1. Sign into the AWS console, click on **Route 53**, and then click on **Hosted zones**.

Route 53 console

2. Select the hosted zone that you want to delete.

Hosted zone console

3. Delete the additional resource record set.

Delete records

4. Confirm to delete the resource record sets.

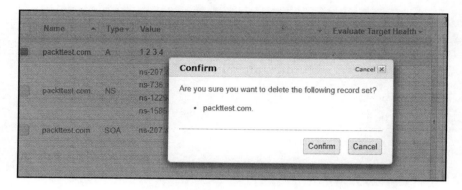

Delete records

5. Then, click on **Back to Hosted Zones**. To delete the hosted zone, click **Delete Hosted Zone**.

Delete hosted zones

6. Confirm to delete the hosted zone.

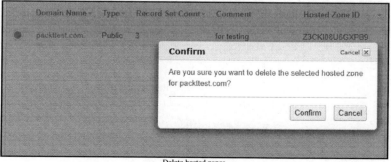

Delete hosted zones

# Creating an Alias record set

ELB, CloudFront, and S3 respond to each request with one or more IP addresses for the environment and change their IP addresses frequently so you cannot directly add the IP address. The only option is to add them as a CNAME record, but CloudFront allows you to add ELB, CloudFront, or S3 as an endpoint while using an **Alias** record.

# How to do it...

Steps to create an Alias record:

1. Select your hosted zone.
2. Click on **Create Record Set** to create a new record.
3. Provide the following values:
    1. **Name**: We will keep it blank, as we want to resolve `test.packttest.com`.
    2. **Type**: Select **A - IPv4 address**.

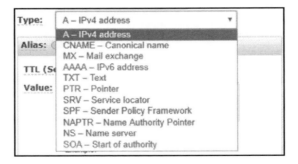

DNS: Resource Record Type

3. **Alias**: select **Yes**.
4. Choose the Alias target from the following:
    * S3 Endpoint
    * ELB Application Load Balancer
    * ELB Classic Load Balancer
    * CloudFront Distributions
    * Elastic Beanstalk
    * Record Sets in the hosted zone

5. Provide the **Alias Hosted Zone ID** (this is specific to selected Alias Target).
6. **Routing Policy**: Select **Simple**.
7. **Evaluate Target Health**: Select **Yes** if you want Route 53 to determine whether to respond to the DNS queries using this resource record set by checking the health of the resource specified by Alias Target.
8. Click **Create**.

# There's more...

- You cannot set the TTL for the following resource set when using it with Alias; Amazon Route 53 uses the CloudFront, Elastic Beanstalk, Elastic Load Balancing, or Amazon S3 Bucket endpoint.
- If your resource record sets points to another resource record set in the same hosted zone using an alias, then Route 53 uses the TTL of the origin resource record set.
- Alias resource record sets can save time because Amazon Route 53 automatically recognizes changes in the resource record sets.
- If the IP address of the load balancer or CloudFront changes, Amazon Route 53 will automatically reflect those changes in DNS queries.
- An alias resource record set is only followed inside Amazon Route 53. This means that both the alias resource record set and its target must be a part of the Amazon resources.
- Amazon Route 53 doesn't charge for alias queries to CloudFront distributions, Elastic Beanstalk environments, ELB load balancers, or Amazon S3 buckets.

# Creating a private hosted zone

A private hosted zone holds information about how you want to route traffic for a domain and its subdomain within a VPC. While creating a private hosted zone, you can only specify a single VPC, however, you can add VPC's into your hosted zone later.

# Getting ready

You need to have a VPC in any region before creating a private hosted zone. To enable private zone functionality, you must set the following values to `True`:

- `enableDnsHostnames`
- `enableDnsSupport`

# How to do it...

1. Sign in to the AWS console and click on **Route 53**.
2. Select **Get started now** under **DNS Management**.
3. Choose **Create Hosted Zone**.
4. Provide the **Domain Name**.
5. Give some informative **Comment**.
6. Select **Type** as **Private Hosted zone for Amazon VPC**.

DNS: Private Hosted Zone creation

7. In the **VPC ID** list, select the VPC ID that you want to associate with the hosted zone.

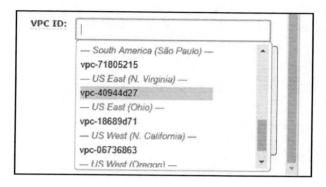

Provide VPC Details

8. Click on **Create** after completion.

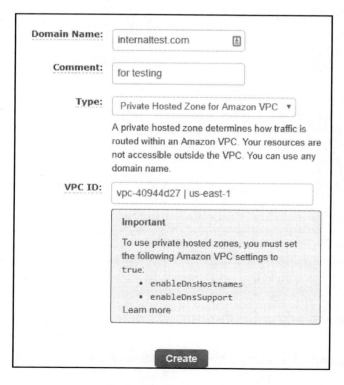

Complete Private Hosted Zone Creation

9. To create an additional VPC within the new hosted zone, click on **Back to Hosted Zones** in the left-hand corner.

Hosted Zone console

10. Click on the radio button to select the hosted zone.

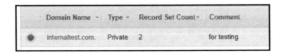

Select Hosted Zone

11. Enter another VPC ID that you want to associate and click on **Associate New VPC**.

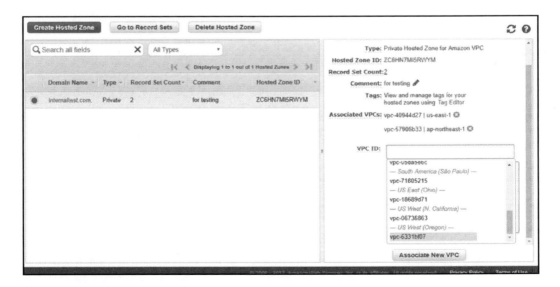

Add another VPC

# There's more...

- You can have more than one hosted zone pointing to the same VPC with a condition that the TLD name should be different.
- The VPC CIDR IP network should not conflict
- You can leverage a simple AD directory:
    - If you want to integrate your on-premise network with your VPC
    - If you want your on-premises network to resolve the domain names and resources in your private hosted zone

# Working with the weighted routing policy

The weighted routing policy can be applied when there are multiple resources that perform the same function, for example, web servers serving the same site from different web servers. Weighted resource record sets let you associate multiple resources with a single DNS name.

Common use cases of the weighted routing policy are as follows:

- Load Balancing
- A/B Testing

# How to do it...

1. Log in to the AWS console, go to **Route 53**, then click on **Hosted zones** and select your hosted zone.

Hosted Zone console

2. Click on **Create Record Set**.
3. Create the first record set, provide the record details, and **Name** as
   test.internaltest.com.

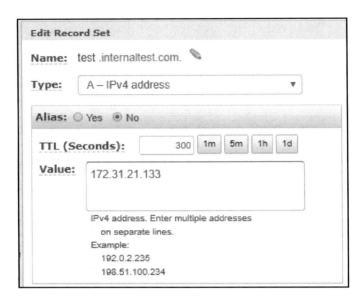

Provide Primary Record Details

4. Select **Routing Policy** as **Weighted**, enter **Weight** as 1, enter a short unique
   description, and **Set ID** as **t2 instance**.

 This will be your unique identifier between the same record sets.

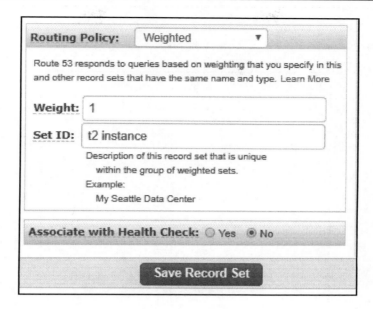

Primary Record Routing Policy

5. Create a second record set, provide record details and **Name** as
   `test.internaltest.com.`

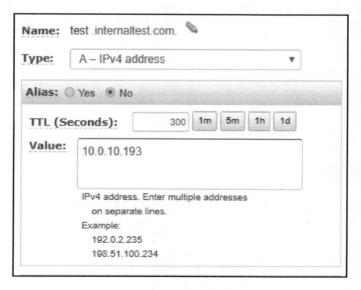

Provide Secondary Record Details

6. Select **Routing Policy** as **Weighted**, enter **Weight** as 4, enter a short unique description, and **Set ID** as **large instance**.

Secondary Record Routing Policy

7. This will create two resource record sets having a weighted routing policy.

Record details with their weight

# How it works...

- Weighted resource record sets contain a group of resources having the same combination of DNS name and type, and each resource record set is assigned a unique identifier and a relative weight.
- Route 53 selects one endpoint from the group. The probability of selecting a resource depends on the weight as a proportion of the total weight of all resources.

- For example: Suppose you have a small on-premises infrastructure and large instances in AWS, to balance your load, you can create two resource record sets with weight 1 (20%) pointing to the on-premises server and weight 4 (80%) pointing to the AWS instances.

# Working with the failover routing policy and health checks

The failover routing policy is a method for routing traffic away from unhealthy resources and to healthy resources. When you have more than one resource performing the same function, for example, more than one web server or application server, you can configure Amazon Route 53 health checks to check the health of your resources and configure the resource record sets in your hosted zone to route traffic only to healthy resources.

## How to do it...

1. Log in to the AWS console and go to **Route 53**.
2. Set up the health check as follows:
   1. Select **Health checks** from the navigation pane and click on **Create health check**.

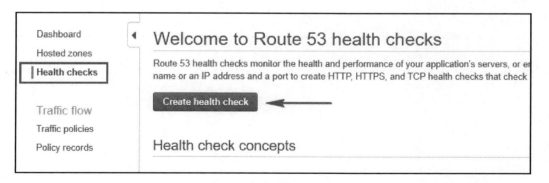

DNS: Health Check console

2. Provide the details as mentioned in the following image and click on **Next**.

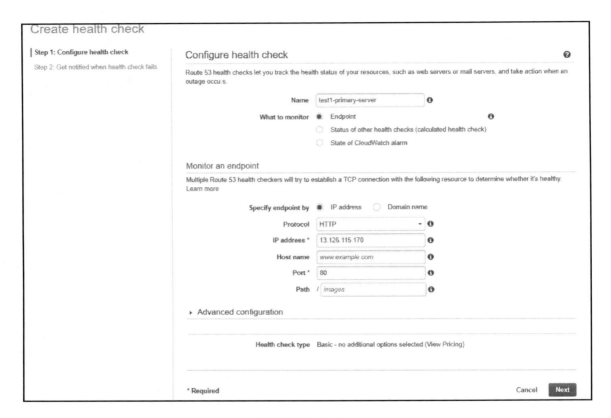

Health Check Configurations

3. Provide **Advanced configuration** if required.

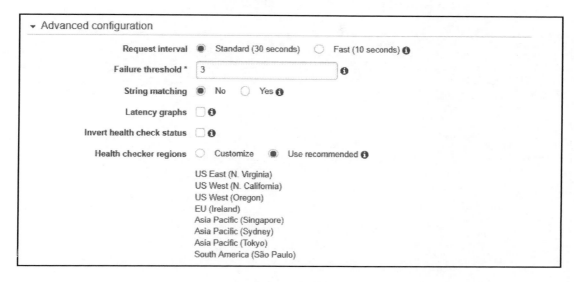

Health Check Advanced Configurations

4. Click **Yes** to set up an alarm.

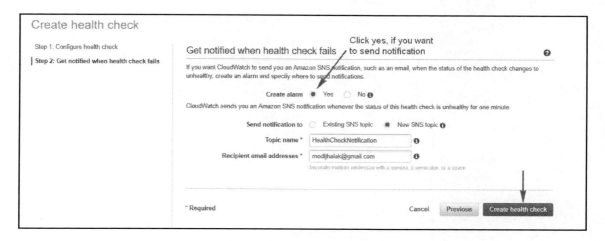

Health Check Alarm setup

5. Make sure the resource is in a **Healthy** state; sometimes it can take a few minutes to come into a **Healthy** state.

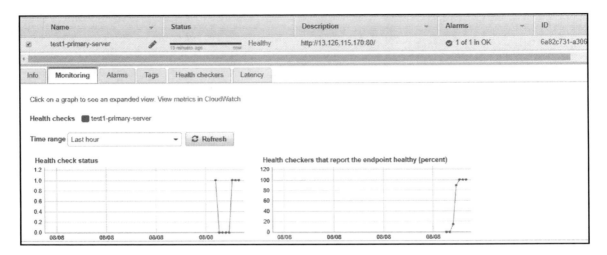

Resource Health Status

6. In the same way, set up a health check for the secondary host.

3. Set up a hosted zone as follows:

  1. Click on **Hosted zones**, select your hosted zone, and click on **Create Record Set**.

  2. Provide the **Name** and **Value** of your resource record set.

Hosted Zone: Create Record

3. Select **Routing Policy** as **Failover**, **Failover Record Type** as **Primary**, **Set ID** as **test1-Primary**, and **Associate with Health Check** as **Yes**.

4. For **Health Check to Associate**, select the health check we just created.

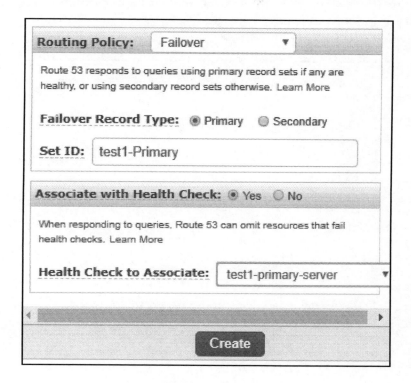

Primary Record Routing Policy

5. In the same way, create a resource record set for the secondary host.

# How it works...

A failover policy will send all traffic to the server you set as primary for as long as that server is healthy. If the health checks determine that it's failing, traffic will be diverted to the secondary backup resource. We have kept the TTL as 60 seconds so that Route 53 responds to the changed health checks in a faster way.

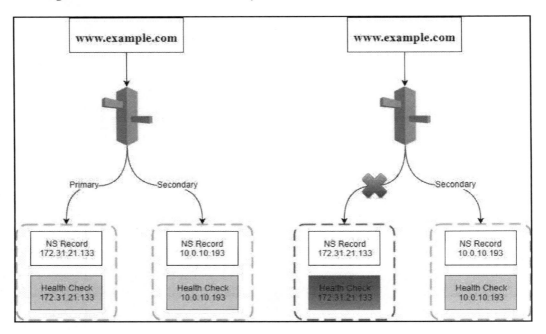

Failover mechanism

# There's more...

- You cannot create health checks for resources in private hosted zone, as health checks are available outside your VPC.
- You can create health checks for public IP/DNS resources.

- If you don't have a public IP attached to your instance, you can create a CloudWatch alarm and set up the health check based on the state of the alarm. For example, CloudWatch sends an alert if the CPU goes above 90% and turns into an alarm state. The health check will react according to the change.

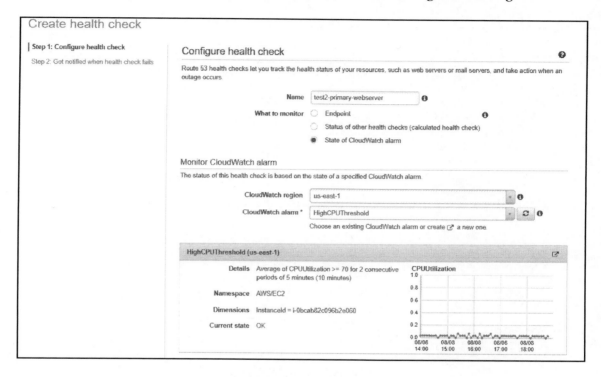

Health Check Setup with Cloudwatch Alarm

- While configuring a failover routing policy, setting up health checks for secondary failover resource record sets is optional.

# 7
# Cloud Security and Network Compliance

In this chapter, we will cover the following recipes:

- Setting up CloudFront--EC2 origin
- Setting up CloudFront--S3 origin
- Geographic restrictions with Amazon CloudFront
- Customizing error responses in CloudFront
- Setting up CloudWatch monitoring
- Setting up ELB and Auto Scaling
- Trusted Advisor
- Protecting log information--sending logs to CloudWatch
- Starting CloudTrail
- Submitting a penetration testing request

## Introduction

Network security is evaluated by each organization making sure it assesses the effectiveness of your defenses. Internet-facing systems receive several hundreds or even millions of attack attempts every day. Many of these are simple scans that our security system can defend against, but others catch you by surprise, unexpectedly shifting into incident investigation and cleanup mode.

This chapter provides assistance in securing a network by explaining important concepts and inter-relationships of security controls.

First of all, we need to understand the shared responsibility model, as infrastructure security is shared between AWS and customer and it varies from different service models of **Infrastructure as a Service (IAAS)**, **Platform as a Service (PAAS)**, and **Software as a Service (SAAS)**.

AWS provides a global infrastructure responsible for the following:

- Underlying hardware
- Physical security
- Network security and compliance
- Virtualization and underlying infrastructure
- Facilities

As a customer, you need to take care of the following:

- OS
- Ingress and outgress traffic from your instance
- AMI hardening and security
- Data in transit and rest
- AWS credentials and **single sign on (SSO)**
- IAM user policies and roles

Here is a simplified diagram to explain the shared responsibility model:

- Customers are responsible for their security and compliance **IN** the Cloud
- AWS is responsible for the security **OF** the Cloud

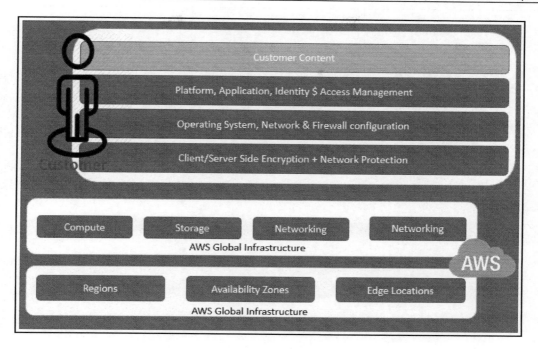

AWS Shared Responsibiliy Model

As AWS takes care of the underlying setup, it allows you to scale and innovate while maintaining a secure environment.

# Types of attack

Here we will be looking at various types of attacks and how to mitigate them with the help of different AWS services:

- **Distributed Denial of Service (DDoS)**: This is a malicious attempt based on bandwidth or resource consumption. DDOS attacks can cause harm without even modifying or touching the intended victim:
    - **Network consumption**: Attackers flood your environment with a large volume of spoofed packets to consume all your network bandwidth.
    - **Resource consumption**: These attempts can sometimes be so strong that they target the vital resources of your system such as CPU cycles, hard disk space, and so on.

- **Peer identity compromise/identity spoofing/man-in-the-middle**: Hackers try to listen to traffic between two network nodes, looking for passwords, password hashes, and program instructions.
- **IP/DNS spoofing**: Attackers try to impersonate a user, device, or client to directly attack the host.
- **Port scanning**: The attacker tries to connect to a selected port or sometimes all ports to exploit the environment. The attacker works in the series of your system to understand the weakness.

Here are some best practices:

- Always use a Security Group
- Set up a Network ACL
- Use IPSec or Direct Connect for trusted connections
- Protect data in transit and rest
- Turn on VPC flow logs
- Always transfer data via SSL/TLS endpoints
- Ensure regular reviews of security controls and policies.

# Setting up CloudFront--EC2 origin

CloudFront is a **Content Delivery Network (CDN)** service provided by AWS. CloudFront offers a globally distributed network which serves cache content such as images, videos, and static files from distributed data centers called **edge locations**. The edge locations are **points of presence (POP)**, which are owned and operated by CloudFront.

While a number of techniques can be used to mitigate DoS/DDoS attacks in the cloud, CloudFront is one of the best services that can manage large user requests while delivering good services to good customers. CloudFront absorbs DoS/DDoS flooding attacks.

There are two types of distribution that CloudFront provides:

- **Web distributions:** Static and dynamic download content; for example, .html, .css, .php, and image files, using HTTP or HTTPS.
- **RTMP distributions:** Stream media files using Adobe Media Server and the Adobe **Real-Time Messaging Protocol (RTMP)**. An RTMP distribution must use an Amazon S3 bucket as the origin.

# Getting ready

Before creating a CloudFront web distribution:

- Make sure your origin is available. Configure origin servers (S3/web server/load balancer) from which CloudFront gets your files for distribution.
- Upload files to the origin servers. Files, also known as objects, typically include web pages, images, and media files but can be anything that can be served over HTTP.
- Configure the S3 bucket for logging.
- Create a CNAME or alias record. Optionally, you can configure your CloudFront distribution to use a custom domain name.
- Upload your SSL certificate if you want to use a custom certificate.
- Optionally, you can configure your origin server to add headers to the files; the headers indicate how long you want the files to stay in the cache in the CloudFront edge locations. By default, each object stays in an edge location for 24 hours before it expires.
- You will need access to create the CloudFront distribution.

# How to do it...

1. Log in to the **AWS Console**, navigate to **Network & Content Delivery**, and then select **CloudFront**.

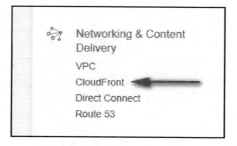

Select CloudFront

2. Navigate to **Distributions** and click on **Create Distribution**.

Create CloudFront Distribution

3. After that, click on **Select delivery method** | **Web** | **Get Started**.

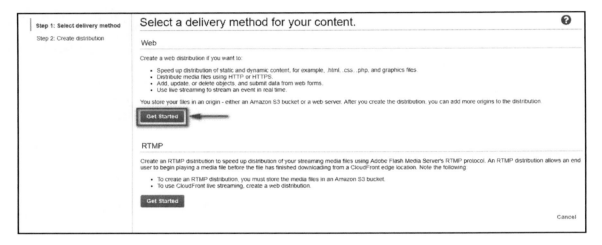

CloudFront Delivery Method

4. Provide an **Origin Domain Name** (here you can provide the EC2 public name/ELB name/domain name as per your requirement).

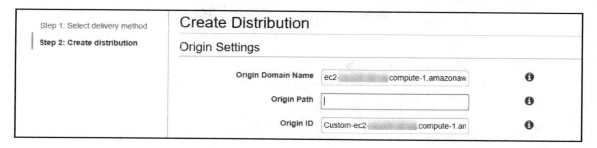

CloudFront: Origin

5. Change as per your specific requirements. I'll be using the default values for this testing.

   1. You can consider changing the **Alternate Domain Names (CNAMEs)** if any are available.

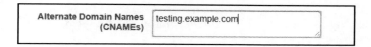

CloudFront: CNAME

   2. Change the **Object Caching** behavior to customize if you want to specify caching expiry in CloudFront. By default, it will take the caching expiry from the headers.

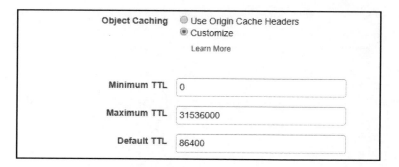

CloudFront: Object Caching

3. Add the **SSL Certificate** if available; otherwise, CloudFront will automatically use the default **\*.cloudfront.net** certificate.

CloudFront: SSL Certificate

6. Set **Logging** as **On**, provide a bucket name in **Bucket for Logs**, and give your folder name in the **Log Prefix**.

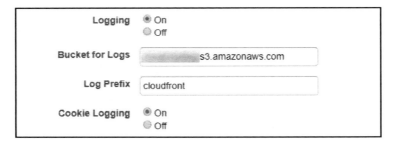

CloudFront: Logs

7. The entire web page will look like the following. Click on **Create Distribution**.

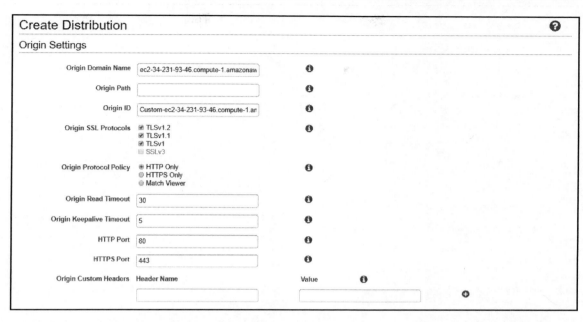

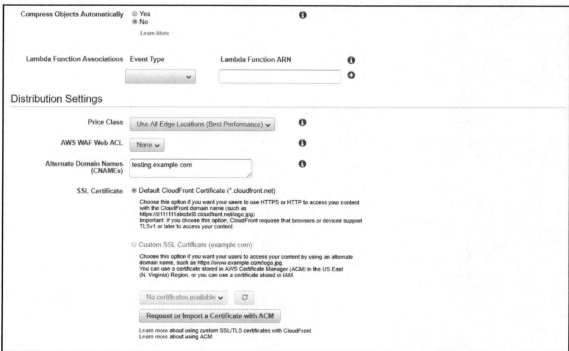

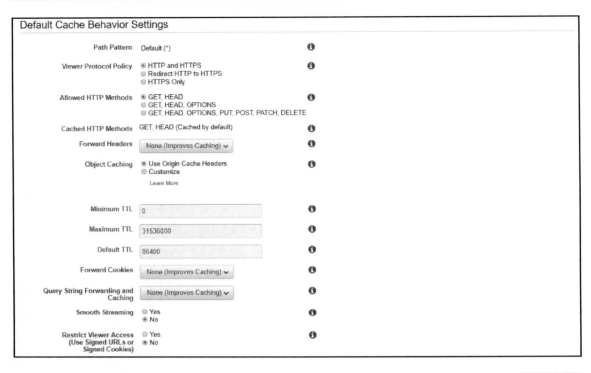

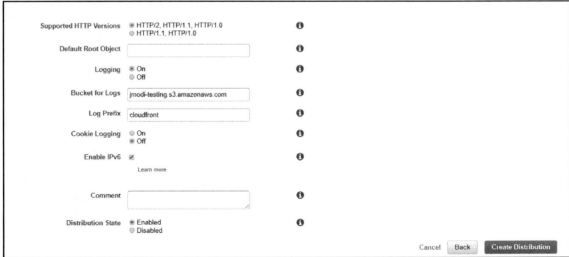

CloudFront: Web Distribution Details

8. Creating the distribution generally takes 15-20 mins.

9. Once the distribution is available, **State** will change to **Enabled**. Click on the ID to get the CloudFront domain name.

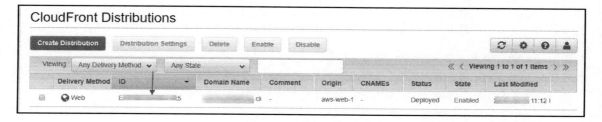

CloudFront Web Distribution

10. You can use the **Domain Name** to visit your web page.

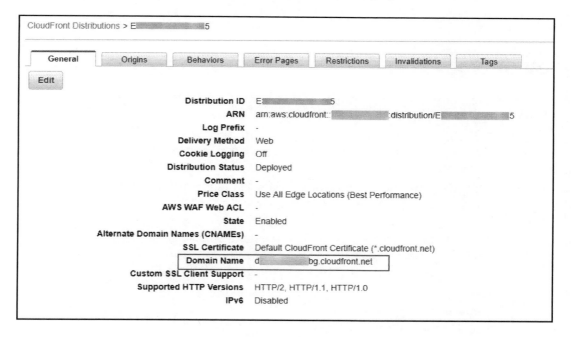

CloudFront Domain Name Details

11. To modify the details or add another behavior, go to **Behaviors** and click on **Create Behavior**.
    1. Note that the behavior decides which data will be served by CloudFront and which data will be served by the origin server.

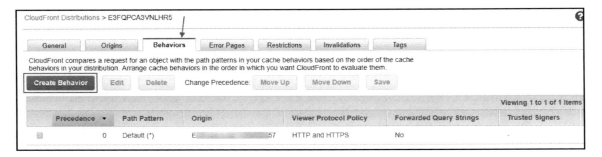

CloudFront Behavior

# How it works...

1. A user accesses your website or application and requests for one or more objects, such as an image file and an HTML file.
2. DNS routes the request to the CloudFront edge location that can best serve the user's request, typically the nearest CloudFront edge location in terms of latency, and routes the request to that edge location.
3. In the edge location, CloudFront checks its cache for the requested files:
    1. If the files are in the cache, CloudFront returns them to the user.
    2. If the files are not available, CloudFront sends the request to the origin server based on the file type. For example, to your Amazon S3 bucket for image files and to your HTTP server, for the HTML files. Then it stores the files to the edge location for the specified duration.
4. Attackers trying to access content from an edge location don't get the details of the end server (S3 or IP of your HTTP server) as the data will be delivered with one of the CloudFront's IP addresses.
5. In the case of attack, CloudFront absorbs the requests, leaving minimal or no impact to your website.

# There's more...

- CloudFront sends your distribution's configuration (but not your content) to all of its edge locations.
- The number of files that you can serve per distribution is unlimited.
- As you develop your website or application, you use the domain name that CloudFront provides for your URLs.
- CloudFront creates reports based on the access log's data. It gives the following reports:
    - CloudFront cache statistics reports:
        - Total requests
        - Percentage of viewer requests by result type
        - Bytes transferred to viewers
        - HTTP status codes
        - Shows viewer GET
    - CloudFront popular objects report
    - CloudFront top referrers report
    - CloudFront usage reports:
        - Number of requests
        - Data transferred by protocol
        - Data transferred by destination
    - CloudFront viewers reports:
        - Devices
        - Browsers
        - Operating systems
        - Locations

# Setting up CloudFront--S3 origin

It is one of the best practices to store your static files (such as text, images, and videos) into S3 and using CloudFront you can distribute the content from S3. In this recipe, we will focus on how to create a CloudFront web distribution for S3 origin.

# How to do it...

1. Create an S3 bucket:
   1. Log in to the **AWS Console**, select **Amazon S3**, and choose **Create bucket**.

S3: Create Bucket

   2. In the **Create Bucket** dialog, enter the name of the bucket, then in **Region**, select a Region for your bucket, and click on **Create**.

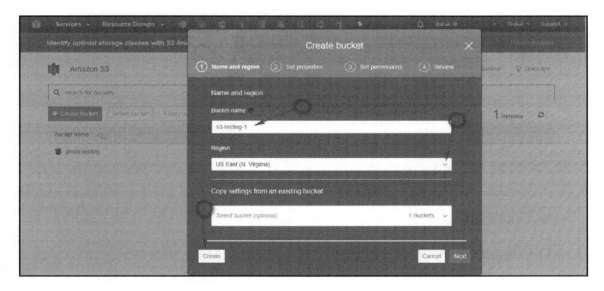

S3 Bucket Details

1. Note that for your bucket to work with CloudFront, the name must conform to the DNS naming requirements. For more information, go to **Bucket Restrictions and Limitations** in the Amazon S3 Developer Guide or visit: `http://docs.aws.amazon.com/AmazonS3/latest/dev/BucketRestrictions.html`

2. By default, Amazon S3 creates buckets in the **US-Standard** region. We recommend that you choose a region close to you to optimize latency, minimize costs, and address regulatory requirements.

3. Select your bucket in the **Buckets** pane and choose **Upload**.

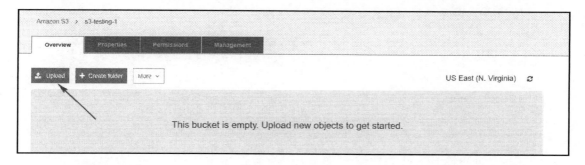

S3 Upload Object

4. On the **Upload** tab, select the files page, choose **Add more files**, and choose the files that you want to upload. Click on **Upload** after completion.

S3 Upload Image

2. Create a CloudFront web distribution as follows:
    1. Open the CloudFront console at `https://console.aws.amazon.com/cloudfront/` and choose **Create Distribution**.
    2. On **Select a delivery method** for your content page in the **Web** section, click on **Get Started**.
    3. On the **Create Distribution** page under **Origin Settings**, choose the Amazon S3 bucket that you created earlier.

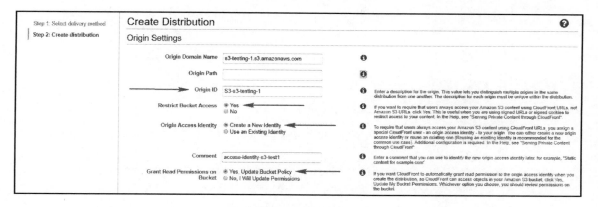

CloudFront: Origin Details

4. Keep all other configurations as default or use the settings provided in recipe 1 (*Setting up CloudFront--EC2 origin*).
5. After all the setups, click **Create Distribution**.
6. After CloudFront has created your distribution, the value of the **Status** column for your distribution will change from **InProgress** to **Deployed**. If you chose to enable the distribution, it will then be ready to process requests.

 This should take less than 15 minutes. The domain name that CloudFront assigns to your distribution appears in the list of distributions. (It also appears on the General tab for a selected distribution.)

3. Test your links-- if your object location in S3 is `https://s3-us-west-2.` `amazonaws.com/bucket-name/file-name` then your CloudFront path will be `http://abc1234abcdef8.cloudfront.net/file-name`.

 If your domain name was `abc1234abcdef8.cloudfront.net` and your object was `image.jpg`, the URL for the link would be: `http://d111111abcdef8.cloudfront.net/image.jpg`. If your object is in a folder within your bucket, include the folder in the URL. For example, if `image.jpg` is located in an images folder, then the URL would be: `d111111abcdef8.cloudfront.net/images/image.jpg`

## There's more...

Restrictions on using alternate domain names include:

- You should have the permission to create a CNAME or alias record with your DNS provider.
- The alternative name should be unique with all the CloudFront distributions.
- As a DNS protocol limitation, you cannot create a CNAME record for the top node of a DNS namespace (for example: `abc.com`) known as the **zone apex**, but you can create CNAME records for `www.abc.com`, `new.abc.com`, and so on.
- If you're using Amazon Route 53 as your DNS service, you can create an alias resource record set instead of a CNAME. With an alias resource record set, you don't pay for Amazon Route 53 queries.
- In addition, you can create an alias resource record set for a domain name at the zone apex (`abc.com`).

# Geographic restrictions with Amazon CloudFront

CloudFront has added a geo-restriction feature to make it easier to restrict access to your content based on the geographic location of your viewers.

# How to do it...

1. Log in to the **AWS Console**, select **CloudFront Distributions,** then select your distribution, and go to the **Restrictions** tab.

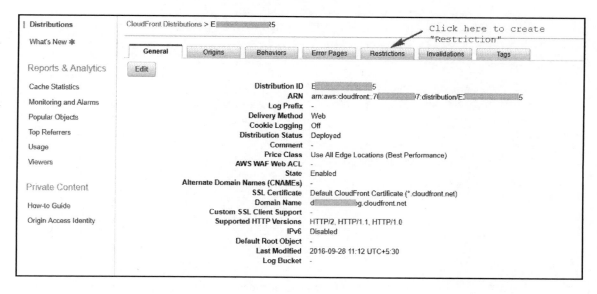

CloudFront Console

2. Click on **Edit.**

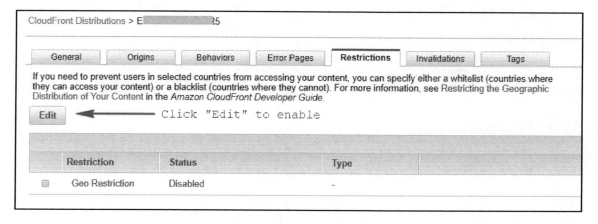

CloudFront Restrictions Setup

Once you enable the feature, you can select whether you want to configure a whitelist or blacklist of countries for your distribution.

3. Select one or more countries from the list in the left-side box, and move those countries to the right-side box and then click on **Yes, Edit** button.

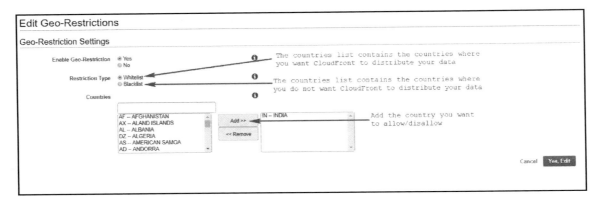

Enable CloudFront Restrictions

4. That's it! Once this configuration gets deployed to our worldwide edge locations (which takes a few minutes), the CloudFront edge locations will begin blocking users from certain countries based on your configuration.

For users that are blocked, CloudFront will serve an HTTP response of 403 (Forbidden). You also have the ability to configure a custom error page with CloudFront for the 403 response so that you can serve a friendlier message to your users if you want (this is explained in the next recipe--*Customizing error responses in CloudFront*).

# How it works...

Imagine you own an online store and have rights to distribute your products to users in a single country. Therefore you need a way to prevent users from across the globe from accessing your product. You can achieve this by using the Amazon CloudFront geo-restriction feature and whitelist the country where you are allowed to sell your product. Then CloudFront edge locations will first check the location of the viewer (based on their IP address) and only serve the content if the viewer's IP address maps to the whitelisted country. CloudFront uses an out-of-sight geo-IP database to map IP addresses to countries.

There is another scenario where you're a software company and want to restrict the download of your encrypted software products by users in certain territories because of licensing terms. In this scenario, you can configure a blacklist of a single country or countries using the CloudFront Management Console (or CLI/API) so that CloudFront edge locations don't serve your content to any requests from one of your blacklisted countries.

# Customizing error responses in CloudFront

The objects that you're serving through CloudFront can be unavailable for a variety of reasons. These reasons fall into two broad categories:

- **Client errors (status code range 4xx):** These errors are the result of HTTP requests sent by the client. For example, the object name isn't available, or the user doesn't have the permissions required to read the object.
- **Server errors (status code range 5xx):** These errors indicate a problem with the origin server as is not able to process the request. For example, the HTTP server is busy or unavailable.

## Getting ready

The HTTP status codes for which CloudFront can return a custom error page includes the following:

- 400, 403, 404, 405, 414
- 500, 501, 502, 503, 504

# How to do it...

1. Log in to the **AWS Console**, select **CloudFront**, select your distribution, and go to the **Error Pages** tab.

2. Click on **Create Custom Error Response**.

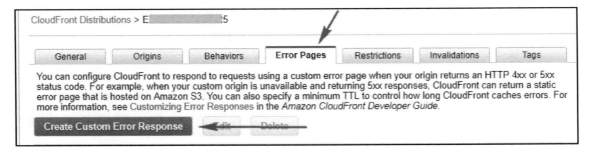

CloudFront: Create Custom Error

3. Set up the error pages and click on **Create**.

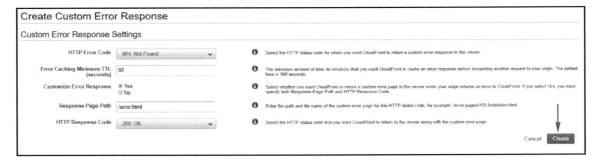

CloudFront: Create Custom Error

# How it works...

When you request for an object or HTTP web page:

1. CloudFront checks for the object in its local cache.
2. If not available, CloudFront checks for the object with the origin server.
3. If the object is unavailable with the origin server as well, your web server will return an HTTP status code to CloudFront.
4. For example, if a user asks for an invalid URL/object, your web server returns a 404 status code to CloudFront, and CloudFront returns the same to the user.
5. You can display a brief and sparsely formatted default message or a web page stating: **Not Found: "The requested URL /myfilename.html was not found on this server"**.
6. You can also specify an image/HTML page having the same formatting as the rest of your website. CloudFront will return an object or HTML file to the viewer that contains your custom error message.

# Setting up CloudWatch monitoring

Think of a scenario where you typically expect 5,000 concurrent sessions to your website at a specific time in a day. Immediately you get to know that the website becomes unresponsive and you find that the traffic has already exceeded twice the amount (10,000). Here you need a solution which monitors your system (Amazon CloudWatch) and triggers an alarm (Amazon SNS) if the current number of concurrent sessions exceeds twice that amount. Immediately, your infrastructure should be in a state to handle the heavy traffic to support good customers.

CloudWatch has the following features:

- It is a monitoring service
- It watches the resources and application you run on AWS
- It collects, processes raw data, and shows real-time metrics
- It collects and monitors log files
- It sets alarms
- It reacts to changes in your environment

EC2 by default sends metric data to CloudWatch every 5 minutes but we can enable detailed monitoring to send metrics every minute.

# Getting ready

In this recipe, we will create a monitoring alert for CPU utilization and send an email to the appropriate recipient. Similarly, you can create an alert for various other resources and can also create custom metrics to monitor.

To create metrics and send a notification, you will need access to CloudWatch and SNS (to send emails).

# How to do it...

Create an alarm and send the notification:

1. Log in to the **AWS Console**, then navigate to **Management Tools**, and select **CloudWatch**.

Select CloudWatch

2. Go to **Alarms** and click on **Create Alarm**.

Create Alarm

3. Search for the metrics (here we are selecting **CPUUtilization**). Select the instance and click on **Next**.

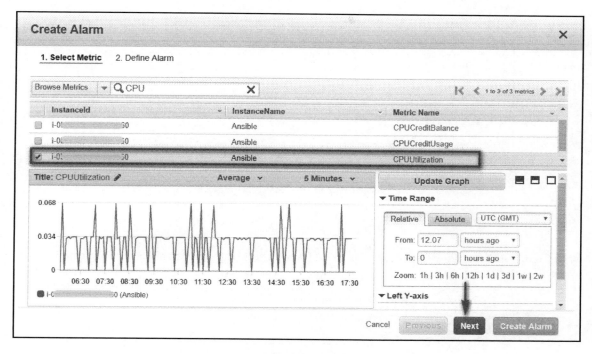

CloudWatch: Metric Details

4. In the **Alarm Threshold** section, provide the unique **Name**, short **Description**, and minimum threshold (that is when you want to trigger an action).

CloudWatch: Alarm Threshold

5.  Provide the **Actions** as given to send an email.

CloudWatch: Alarm Actions

6.  Go through the preview of the **Alarm** in the right corner side and click on **Create Alarm**.

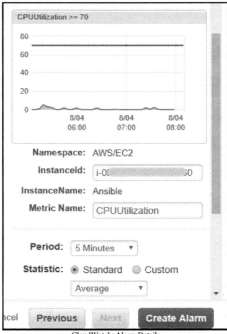

CloudWatch: Alarm Details

7. You will get an email to confirm the subscription. Click on **I will do it later**.

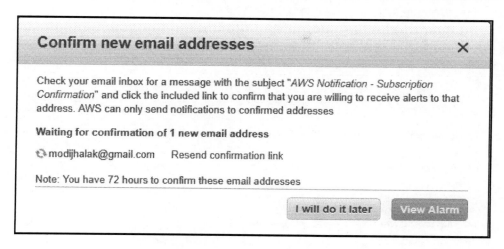

**Confirm new email addresses**                                    ✕

Check your email inbox for a message with the subject "*AWS Notification - Subscription Confirmation*" and click the included link to confirm that you are willing to receive alerts to that address. AWS can only send notifications to confirmed addresses

**Waiting for confirmation of 1 new email address**

🔄 modijhalak@gmail.com    Resend confirmation link

Note: You have 72 hours to confirm these email addresses

                                    I will do it later    View Alarm

CloudWatch: Email setup

8. Your alarm is now available in the pending state.

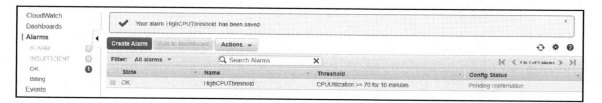

| State | Name | Threshold | Config Status |
|-------|------|-----------|---------------|
| OK | HighCPUThreshold | CPUUtilization >= 70 for 10 minutes | Pending confirmation |

CloudWatch: Alarm Status

9. To confirm the email you have received, click **Confirm subscription**. Check your spam box if you haven't received any email.

 You will not receive any confirmation email if the SNS topic is already created and the alarm status will automatically change.

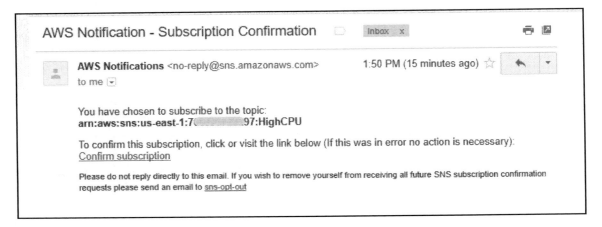

CloudWatch: Email Confirmation

10. Check the state of the alarm again.

# There's more...

You can use CloudWatch to recover or restart the instance automatically whenever you receive Instance/System Status Check Failed.

To recover the instance whenever you receive System Status Check Failed:

1. Follow the same steps until step 2 provided in the last section.
2. Search for **StatusCheckFailed_System** and click on **Next**.

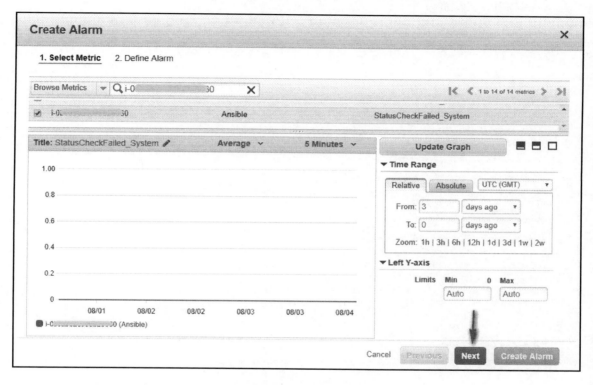

CloudWatch: Status Check Failed Alarm

3. In the **Actions** pane, click on **+EC2 Action**, then select the **Recover this instance**, and click on **Create Alarm**.

CloudWatch: Status Check Failed Alarm Action

4. To restart the instance whenever you receive Instance Status Check Failed:
   - Follow the same steps until step 2 provided in the last section
   - Search for **StatusCheckFailed_Instance** and click on **Next**
   - In the **Actions** pane, click on **+EC2 Action**, then select **Reboot this instance** and click on **Create Alarm**

# Setting up ELB and Auto Scaling

Along with conventional approaches for DoS/DDoS attack mitigation and protection, the AWS cloud provides capabilities based on its elasticity. DoS/DDoS attacks are attempts to deplete limited compute, memory, disk, or network resources, which often work against on-premises infrastructure. However, the AWS cloud is elastic, in the sense that new resources can be employed on demand, if and when required.

## How to do it...

Steps to create ELB and Auto Scaling have already been shared in Chapter 3, *VPC Advanced Components*.

## How it works...

As AWS services are highly durable in nature, you can have ELB and ASG in the case of an attack:

- All the requests will come to your Elastic Load Balancing and beneath that, it will go to your EC2 servers.
- You can configure CloudWatch to react on the sudden spikes (For example, trigger an alarm and send SNS notification or trigger EC2 instances using Auto Scaling).
- Auto Scaling will scale out your web server based on the load or number of requests.
- This will give you some time to fight against the attack by serving data to good users. Even under heavy attack, the web servers could scale to perform and provide optimal user experience by leveraging cloud elasticity.
- Auto Scaling will shrink back when the attack stops.

# Trusted Advisor

AWS Trusted Advisor helps you to optimize your infrastructure by giving real-time guidance by comparing your current infrastructure with AWS best practices, reducing cost, increasing performance, improving security, and fault tolerance.

AWS compares the best practices in the following four categories:

- Cost optimization
- Performance
- Security
- Fault tolerance

# Getting ready

In this recipe, we will go through the AWS Trusted Advisor console and use Amazon CloudWatch events to detect and react to changes in the status of Trusted Advisor checks.

You will need access to Trusted Advisor, CloudWatch, and SNS to perform this recipe.

# How to do it...

1. Log in to the **AWS Console**, navigate to **Management Tools**, and click on **Trusted Advisor**.

Trusted Advisor

2. It will take some time to perform the checks and it then gives the following screen:

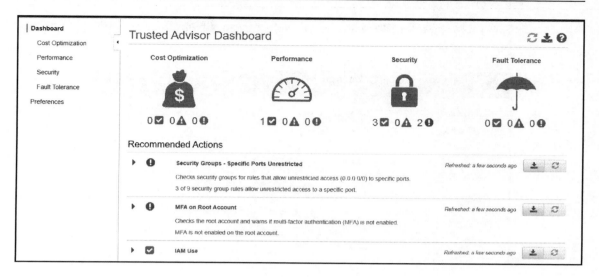

Trusted Advisor Console

3. In the **Recommended Actions** section, select the warning and on the basis of **Alert Criteria**, you can take the required action.

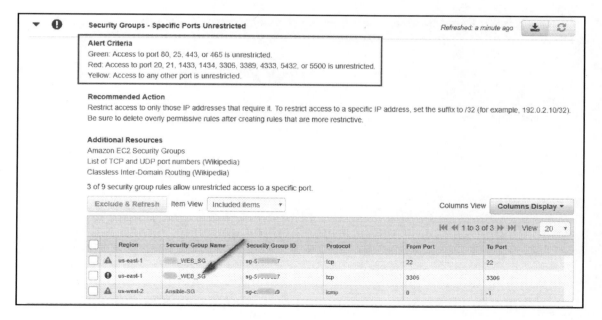

Trusted Advisor Alerts

4. Now go to the **CloudWatch** console, select **Events** from the navigation pane, and click on **Create rule**.

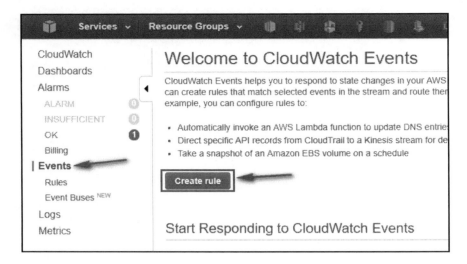

CloudWatch Events

5. Under **Event Source**, select **Service Name** as **Trusted Advisor**.
   1. Select **Event Type** as **All Events**.

 Be wise while choosing this option, as this can flood emails into your mailbox.

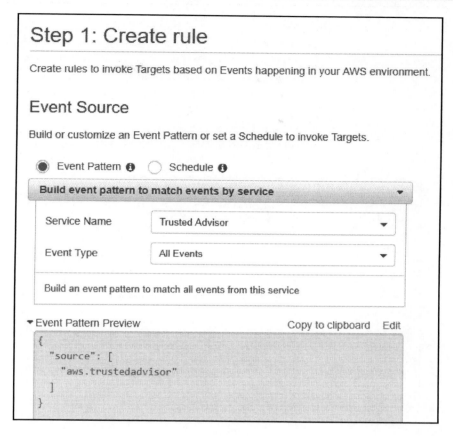

CloudWatch Event Rule

2. For specific events:
   1. **Status values**: Select **Check Item Refresh Status** in **Event Type** and choose **Specific Status(es)** as ERROR and WARN.
   2. **Trusted Advisor checks**: Choose **Specific check(s)** and then choose one or more check names from the list.
   3. **AWS resources**: Choose **Specific resource ID(s)** by ARN, and then type the ARNs of the resources (or select **Any resource ID to apply rules to all resources**).

CloudWatch Events Details

6. In the **Targets** area, click **Add Target**.
7. Select the **Target Type** (which action you want to perform), select **SNS topic**, select the **Topic** that you have created, and in **Configure input** select **Matched event**.

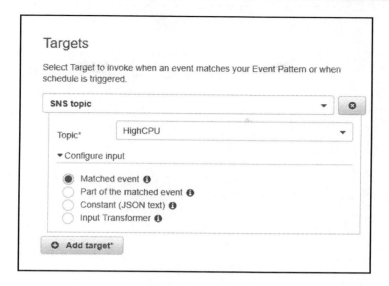

CloudWatch Events Targets

8. Click on **Configure details**.

CloudWatch Event Configure Details

9. In the section **Step 2: Configure rule details**, under **Rule definition** provide the **Name** and **Description** and click on **Create rule**.

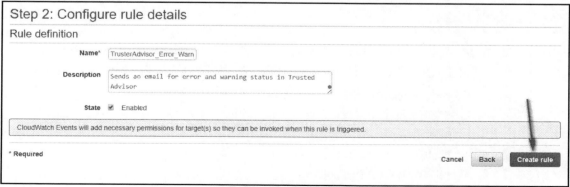

CloudWatch Events Configure Rule

10. Once created, it should give a green status.

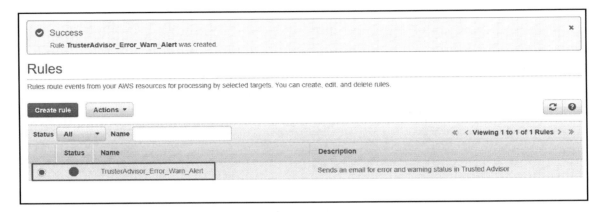

CloudWatch Events Rule Status

# How it works...

Trusted Advisor scans your environment and compares it with the AWS best practices. Once the scan is done, it provides recommended actions. You can take actions by selecting the specified links.

Further, we have created AWS CloudWatch events to send alerts for any changes in Trusted Advisor.

# Protecting log information--sending logs to CloudWatch

For critical applications, all add, change/modify, and delete activities or transactions must generate a log entry. Each log entry should contain the following information:

- User identification information
- Type of event
- Date and time stamp
- Success or failure indication
- Origination of event
- Identity or name of the affected data, system component, or resource

Protecting logs:

- Verify that audit trails are enabled and active for system components
- Ensure that only individuals who have a job-related need can view audit trail files
- Confirm that the current audit trail files are protected from unauthorized modifications via access control mechanisms, physical segregation, and/or network segregation
- Ensure that the current audit trail files are promptly backed up to a centralized log server or media that is difficult to alter
- Verify that regular log reviews are performed for all system components

# Getting ready

Think of a scenario where you want to give access of your logs to your security team without them logging into the server and creating a separate log server can be little expensive.

CloudWatch logs give you the ability to monitor and troubleshoot your systems and applications, and custom log files. You can ship your logs to CloudWatch and monitor them in near real time, for specific phrases, values, or patterns.

For example, you can set up an alarm on specific errors based on your system logs (such as, user log in failed) or view graphs based on your application logs (such as, the latency of web requests). These alarms or graphs will not manipulate the original files, so you can check logs any time to get more insights. Logs files are stored securely and can be accessed for up to 10 years, so you don't have to worry about filling up hard drives.

The CloudWatch Logs Agent is supported on Amazon Linux, Ubuntu, and Windows. This agent will support the ability to monitor individual log files on the host.

# How to do it...

1. Configure your IAM role or user for CloudWatch logs as follows:
    1. Open the IAM console at `https://console.aws.amazon.com/iam/`.
    2. In the navigation pane, click **Roles**, and then on the **Role Name** column, click on **IAM role**.
    3. Under **Inline Policies**, click **Create Role Policy**.
    4. On the **Set Permissions** page, click **Custom Policy**, and then click **Select**.
    5. On the **Review Policy** page, in the **Policy Name** field, type a name for the policy.

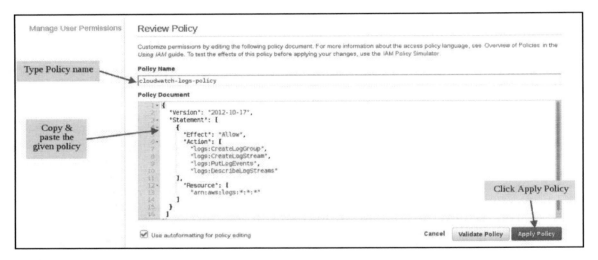

IAM Policy

6. In the **Policy Document** field, paste the following policy:

```
{
"Version": "2012-10-17",
"Statement": [
{
"Effect": "Allow",
"Action": [
"logs:CreateLogGroup",
"logs:CreateLogStream",
"logs:PutLogEvents",
"logs:DescribeLogStreams"
```

```
],
"Resource": [
"arn:aws:logs:*:*:*"
]
}
]
}
```

7. Click on **Apply Policy**.

2. Install and configure CloudWatch logs on an existing Amazon EC2 instance:
    1. Connect to your EC2 instance.
    2. The CloudWatch Logs agent installer requires certain information during set up. Before you start, you will need to know what log file you want to monitor and its timestamp format. You should also have the following information ready:
        1. **AWS access key ID**: Press *Enter* if you are using an IAM role. Otherwise, enter your AWS access key ID.
        2. **AWS secret access key**: Press *Enter* if you are using an IAM role. Otherwise, enter your AWS secret access key.
        3. **Default region name**: Press *Enter*. The default is us-east-1. You can set this to us-east-1, us-west-1, us-west-2, eu-west-1, eu-central-1, ap-southeast-1, ap-southeast-2, or ap-northeast-1.
        4. **Default output format**: Leave blank and press *Enter*.
        5. **Path of log file to upload**: This is the location of the file that contains the log data you want to send. The installer will suggest a path for you.
        6. **Destination log group name**: This is the name for your log group. The installer will suggest a log group name for you.
        7. **Destination log stream name**: By default, this is the name of the host. The installer will suggest a hostname for you.
        8. **Timestamp format**: Specify the format of the timestamp within the specified log file. Choose custom to specify your own format.
        9. **Initial position**: This is how the data will be uploaded. Set this to start_of_file to upload everything in the data file. Set it to end_of_file to upload only newly appended data.

3. Run the CloudWatch Logs agent installer. On the instance, open a command prompt, type the following commands, and then follow the prompts:

```
[root@ip-172-31-45-203 ~]# cd /home/centos/
 [root@ip-172-31-45-203 jhalak]# wget
https://s3.amazonaws.com/aws-CloudWatch/downloads/latest/aw
slogs-agent-setup.py
 [root@ip-172-31-45-203 jhalak]# python ./awslogs-agent-
setup.py --region us-west-2
 Launching interactive setup of CloudWatch Logs agent ...
 Step 1 of 5: Installing pip ...DONE
 Step 2 of 5: Downloading the latest CloudWatch Logs agent
bits ... DONE
 Step 3 of 5: Configuring AWS CLI ...
 AWS Access Key ID [***************A6GQ]:
//Press Enter
 AWS Secret Access Key [***************0Y3Q]:
//Press Enter
 Default region name [us-west-2]:
//Press Enter
 Default output format [None]: text
//Press Enter
Step 4 of 5: Configuring the CloudWatch Logs Agent ...
Path of log file to upload [/var/log/messages]:
//Press Enter
 Destination Log Group name [/var/log/messages]:
//Press Enter
 Choose Log Stream name:
  1. Use EC2 instance id.    2. Use hostname.    3. Custom.
 Enter choice [1]:
//Press Enter
 Choose Log Event timestamp format:
  1. %b %d %H:%M:%S     (Dec 31 23:59:59)
  2. %d/%b/%Y:%H:%M:%S (10/Oct/2000:13:55:36)
  3. %Y-%m-%d %H:%M:%S (2008-09-08 11:52:54)
  4. Custom
 Enter choice [1]:
//Press Enter
 Choose initial position of upload:
  1. From start of file.
  2. From end of file.
 Enter choice [1]:
//Press Enter More log files to configure? [Y]: N
//Press Y to configure more logs
 Step 5 of 5: Setting up agent as a daemon ...DONE
 --------------------------------------------------------
```

```
   - Configuration file successfully saved at:
/var/awslogs/etc/awslogs.conf
   - You can begin accessing new log events after a few
moments at
https://console.aws.amazon.com/CloudWatch/home?region=us-we
st-2#logs:
   - You can use 'sudo service awslogs
start|stop|status|restart' to control the daemon.
   - To see diagnostic information for the CloudWatch Logs
Agent, see /var/log/awslogs.log
   - You can rerun interactive setup using 'sudo python
./awslogs-agent-setup.py --region us-west-2 --only-
generate-config'
------------------------------------------------------------
```

4. After you have completed these steps, the installer asks if you want to configure another log file; you can run the process as many times as you like for each log file. If you have no more log files to monitor, choose *N* when prompted by the installer to set up another log.

5. You should see the newly created log group and log stream in the CloudWatch console after the agent has been running for a few moments.

6. To check the status, run the following command:

```
[root@ip-172-31-45-203 jhalak]# systemctl status awslogs
 awslogs.service - LSB: Daemon for AWSLogs agent.
 Loaded: loaded (/etc/rc.d/init.d/awslogs)
 Active: active (running) since ---
 ---- Jul 22 20:10:56 ip-172-31-45-203.us-
west-2.compute.internal systemd[1]: Started LSB: Daemon for
AWSLogs agent..
```

7. To configure more logs with the same setup, run the following command:

```
[root@ip-172-31-45-203 jhalak]# python ./awslogs-agent-
setup.py --region us-west-2 --only-generate-config
Launching interactive setup of CloudWatch Logs agent ...
Skipping downloading and installation of agent bits.Step 3
of 5: Configuring AWS CLI ...
AWS Access Key ID [***************A6GQ]:
// press Enter
AWS Secret Access Key [***************0Y3Q]:
// press Enter
Default region name [us-west-2]:
```

```
// press Enter
Default output format [text]:
// press Enter
Step 4 of 5: Configuring the CloudWatch Logs Agent ...
Path of log file to upload [/var/log/messages]:
/var/log/httpd/access_log              //Enter the required
path
Destination Log Group name [/var/log/httpd/access_log]:
// press Enter
Choose Log Stream name:
1. Use EC2 instance id.
2. Use hostname.
3. Custom.
Enter choice [1]:
//Press Enter
Choose Log Event timestamp format:
1. %b %d %H:%M:%S (Dec 31 23:59:59)
2. %d/%b/%Y:%H:%M:%S (10/Oct/2000:13:55:36)
3. %Y-%m-%d %H:%M:%S (2008-09-08 11:52:54)
4. Custom
Enter choice [1]:
//Press Enter
Choose initial position of upload:
1. From start of file.
2. From end of file.
Enter choice [1]: //Press Enter
More log files to configure? [Y]: N
Step 5 of 5: Setting up agent as a daemon ...DONE
------------------------------------------------------
- Configuration file successfully saved at:
/var/awslogs/etc/awslogs.conf
- You can begin accessing new log events after a few
moments at
https://console.aws.amazon.com/CloudWatch/home?region=us-we
st-2#logs:
- You can use 'sudo service awslogs
start|stop|status|restart' to control the daemon.
- To see diagnostic information for the CloudWatch Logs
Agent, see /var/log/awslogs.log
- You can rerun interactive setup using 'sudo python
./awslogs-agent-setup.py --region us-west-2 --only-
generate-config'
------------------------------------------------------
```

8. To restart the CloudWatch agent, run the following command:

```
[root@ip-172-31-45-203 jhalak]# systemctl daemon-reload
[root@ip-172-31-45-203 jhalak]# systemctl restart awslogs
```

9. To configure the error logs, run the following command:

```
[root@ip-172-31-45-203 jhalak]# python ./awslogs-agent-
setup.py --region us-west-2 --only-generate-config
Launching interactive setup of CloudWatch Logs agent ...
Skipping downloading and installation of agent bits.Step 3
of 5: Configuring AWS CLI ...
AWS Access Key ID [***************A6GQ]:
AWS Secret Access Key [***************0Y3Q]:
Default region name [us-west-2]:
Default output format [text]:
Step 4 of 5: Configuring the CloudWatch Logs Agent ...
Path of log file to upload [/var/log/messages]:
/var/log/httpd/error_log
Destination Log Group name [/var/log/httpd/error_log]:
Choose Log Stream name:
1. Use EC2 instance id.
2. Use hostname.
3. Custom.
Enter choice [1]:
Choose Log Event timestamp format:
1. %b %d %H:%M:%S (Dec 31 23:59:59)
2. %d/%b/%Y:%H:%M:%S (10/Oct/2000:13:55:36)
3. %Y-%m-%d %H:%M:%S (2008-09-08 11:52:54)
4. Custom
Enter choice [1]:
Choose initial position of upload:
1. From start of file.
2. From end of file.
Enter choice [1]:
More log files to configure? [Y]: N
Step 5 of 5: Setting up agent as a daemon ...DONE
------------------------------------------------------------
- Configuration file successfully saved at:
/var/awslogs/etc/awslogs.conf
- You can begin accessing new log events after a few
moments at
https://console.aws.amazon.com/CloudWatch/home?region=us-we
st-2#logs:
- You can use 'sudo service awslogs
start|stop|status|restart' to control the daemon.
- To see diagnostic information for the CloudWatch Logs
```

```
Agent, see /var/log/awslogs.log
- You can rerun interactive setup using 'sudo python
./awslogs-agent-setup.py --region us-west-2 --only-
generate-config'
---------------------------------------------------
```

10. Once done, you can configure more application logs in the same way.

3. Check the logs in the AWS CloudWatch console:

1. Log in to the **AWS Console**, go to **CloudWatch**, and click on the **Logs** tab in the left-side navigation pane.

CloudWatch Logs

2. Now you can see all the logs created.

3. Select the log you have configured /var/log/messages for.

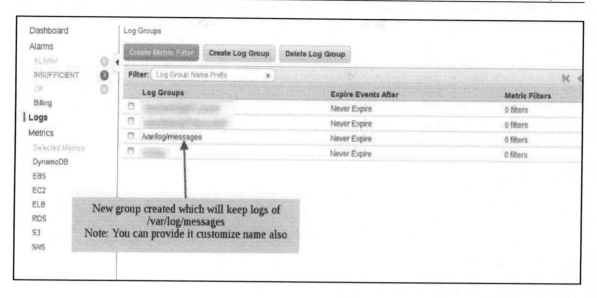

CloudWatch Log Groups

# There's more...

Examples of what you can do with Amazon CloudWatch and your logs are as follows:

- **Real-time application and system monitoring**: You can use CloudWatch logs to monitor applications and systems using log data in near real-time. For example, CloudWatch Logs can track the number of errors that occur in your application logs and send you a notification whenever the rate of errors exceed a threshold that you specify. Amazon CloudWatch uses your log data for monitoring; so no code changes are required.

- **Long-term log retention**: You can use CloudWatch Logs to store your log data for as long as you need in a highly durable and cost-effective storage without worrying about hard drives running out of space. The CloudWatch Logs Agent makes it easy to quickly move both rotated and unrotated log files off of a host and into the log service. You can then access the raw log event data when you need it.

- Limitations of CloudWatch logs:
    - Up to 5 GB of incoming data for free
    - Up to 5 GB of data archiving for free
    - The maximum number of log groups per AWS account is 500
    - The maximum number of metric filters is 100 per log group
    - The maximum event size is 256 KB
    - The maximum batch size is 1 MB
    - The maximum rate of a `PutLogEvents` request is five requests per second per log stream
    - The maximum batch size of a `PutLogEvents` request is 1 MB
    - The maximum rate of a `GetLogEvents` request is 10 requests per second per AWS account

# Starting CloudTrail

Amazon CloudTrail is an API log monitoring and recording tool. CloudTrail captures and records all the API calls and related events for your account and stores it into S3. You can also deliver the logs to CloudWatch logs and events.

CloudWatch primarily does three tasks:

- Stores log files in S3
- Looks up the API history
- Gives notification on specific API activity

You can create two types of trails:

- A trail that applies to all regions
- A trail that applies to one region

# How to do it...

1. Sign in to the **AWS Management Console** and click on **CloudTrail**.

Select CloudTrail

2. Click on **Get Started Now**.

CloudTrail: Get Started

3. On the **Turn on CloudTrail** page, provide the **Trail name** and select **Yes** if you want to **Apply trail to all regions**.

4. Under **Management events**, for **Read/Write events**, choose if you want your trail to log **All**, **Read-only**, **Write-only**, or **None**, and then choose **Save**. By default, trails log **All management events**.

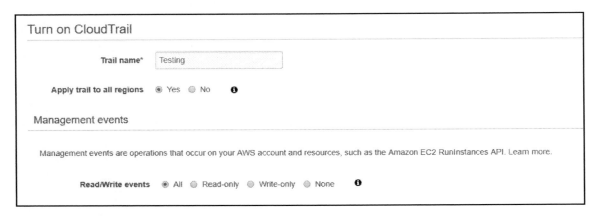

Turn on CloudTrail

5. Provide a storage location, select **Yes**, and provide a name to your bucket. Select **No** if you have an available bucket and provide the bucket name.

S3 bucket for CloudTrail

6. Click on **Advanced** and provide the details shown in the following screenshot:

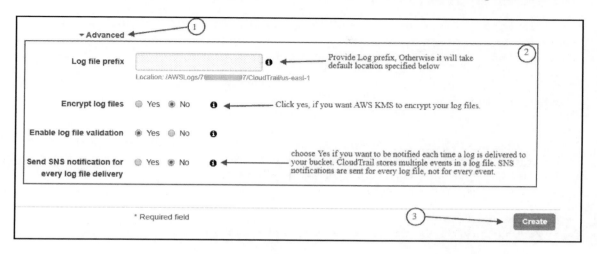

CloudTrail Advanced Details

7. The new trail appears on the **Trails** page. The **Trails** page shows the trails in your account from all regions.

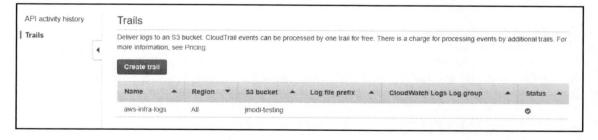

CloudTrail Logs

# How it works...

CloudTrail captures API calls and related events made by or on behalf of an AWS account and delivers log files to an Amazon S3 bucket. CloudTrail pushes log files generally every 5 minutes.

# There's more...

You can integrate CloudTrail with your third-party log monitoring tools such as **Loggly** using the API automate trail creation for your organization, check the status of your trails, and control how administrators turn CloudTrail logging on and off.

By default, log files are encrypted using Amazon S3 **server-side encryption** (SSE). You can store your log files in your bucket for as long as you want. You can also define the Amazon S3 life cycle rules to archive or delete log files automatically.

You can create up to five trails for each region. After you create a trail, CloudTrail automatically starts logging API calls and related events in your account. To stop logging, you can turn off logging for the trail or delete it.

# Submitting a penetration testing request

Penetration testing is a cyber attack against your infrastructure to test exploitable vulnerabilities. The main objective of pen testing is to determine security weakness. AWS considers pen testing as abusive behavior so it, by default, blocks the source IP. Before performing pen testing, you need to inform AWS about the test.

## Getting ready

You can request authorization for penetration testing by signing in with your root account credentials and filling out the **AWS Vulnerability/Penetration Testing Request Form**. AWS will follow up on your request within 2 business days.

You cannot perform pen testing on small/micro/nano EC2 or RDS instances.

# How to do it...

1. Log in to the **AWS Console** using the root account.
2. Click on the URL to open the form: `https://aws.amazon.com/forms/penetration-testing-request`
3. Provide all the required details:
   1. **Contact Information**:

---

### Contact Information

Please provide the email address and the associated name of the AWS account owner with which you have used to log into this form. The AWS Account ID number of the account used to log into this form will be sent along with your submission. If you would like to request testing for a different account, please log out and log back in with the account for which you want to test.

Your Name:*

Company Name*

Email Address

Additional Email Address

Additional Email Address

Additional Email Address

Third Party Contact Information

---

Penetration Testing Form

2. **Scan Information**:

## Scan Information

IP Addresses to be scanned (Destination)*

Are the instances the source of the scan or the target of the scan?*

☐ Source

☐ Target

Instance IDs*

Scanning IP addresses (Source)*

Total Bandwidth (Please provide expected Gbps)*

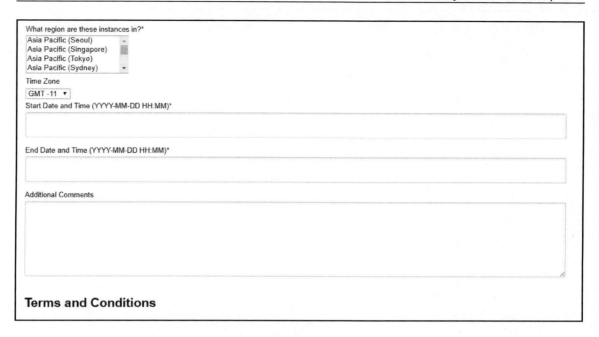

Penetration Testing Form

4. Click **I agree** in the **Terms and Conditions Agreement** section and click on **Submit**.

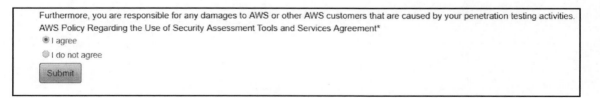

Penetration Testing Form

5. You will get a confirmation email within 2 days.

# 8
# Troubleshooting and VPC Limits

In this chapter, we will cover the following recipes:

- Troubleshooting IP address overlapping
- Errors while connecting an EC2 instance in a VPC
- Internet not accessible in the instance
- Internet not accessible in the private subnet instance (NAT Gateway)
- Not able to delete a VPC
- Enabling VPC flow logs
- Increasing VPC limits

## Introduction

In this chapter, we will go through basic and advanced troubleshooting steps while creating and managing a VPC. You may have your own tools to check such issues, but there are a few standard series of tasks that you can look into. For example, incorrect CIDR block, overlapping routing table, and so on.

# Troubleshooting IP address overlapping

Think of a scenario--you have already set up a VPC with instances inside it with, say, 172.0.x.x/16 CIDR and you've realized that the client who is going to connect also has the same CIDR block. So, wisely choose the IP address ranges for your VPC to avoid conflict with another network that you might connect to.

## Getting ready

You will need access to modify the VPC.

## How to do it...

The only option is to create a new VPC and migrate resources into the new one. Please follow the steps given in `Chapter 2`, *Building Your Own Custom VPC*, to create a new VPC.

## There's more...

You can create multiple VPCs with the same CIDR blocks. These VPCs will act as an individual network, but if you need to do peering between two VPCs, then it will create an issue. As you can't modify a VPC CIDR block, the only solution for this issue is to create another VPC that doesn't overlap with your peering VPC.

# Errors while connecting an EC2 instance in a VPC

There can be multiple reasons for getting such an error; a few of them are mentioned following:

- EC2 created in the wrong subnet group or private subnet
- Instance doesn't have a public IP or you are trying to connect with a private IP
- SSH/RDP port is not opened in the security group or the security group is not attached to the instance

# Getting ready

You should have access to EC2 and VPC to view and modify the resources.

# How to do it...

The following steps are to be followed:

1. Start by checking the IP of the instance. Verify that you are using the correct IP address. Follow the following steps to check the IP:
    1. Log in to the **AWS Console** | **EC2** | **Instances** | **Instance**.

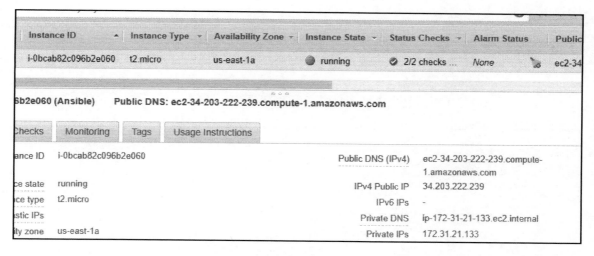

AWS EC2 Console

2. Check that your instance has either a public IP address or an Elastic IP address associated with it in the case of public instances. Follow the following steps to check the Associated Elastic IP:

3. Log in to the **AWS Console** | **EC2** | **Elastic IPs** | **Allocate new address**.

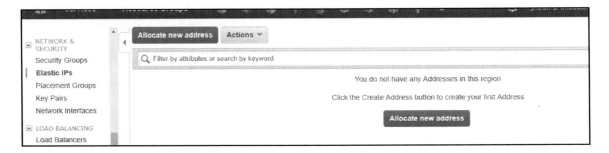

Allocate Elastic IP

4. When prompted, click on **Allocate**.

Allocate Elastic IP

5. Once the IP comes up, go to **Actions** | **Associate address**.

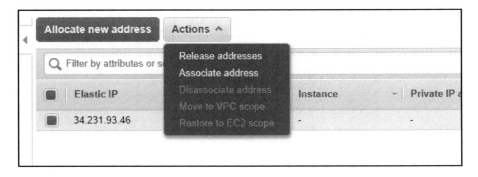

Associate Elastic IP

6. Provide the instance details.

Addresses > Associate address

## Associate address

Select the instance OR network interface to which you want to associate this Elastic IP address (34.231.93.46)

| | |
|---|---|
| Resource type | ◉ Instance   ❶ |
| | ○ Network interface |
| Instance | i-0bcab82c096b2e060   ▾   ↻ |
| Private IP | 172.31.21.133   ▾   ↻ ❶ |
| Reassociation | ☐ Allow Elastic IP to be reassociated if already attached ❶ |

> ⚠ **Warning**
> If you associate an Elastic IP address with your instance, your current public IP address is released. Learn more.

\* Required         Cancel   **Associate**

Associate Elastic IP

7. The Associated IP and details will look like this.

Associate Elastic IP

8. Check the IP in the instance.

AWS EC2 Elastic IP Details

2. Check that both **System Status Checks** and **Instance Status Checks** are cleared. The following are the steps:

    1. Log in to the **AWS Console** | **EC2** | **Instances**.

    2. Then choose the **Status Checks** tab.

    3. Verify that the instance passes both status checks.

3. The SSH/RDP port may not be opened in the Security Group. Or there may be a scenario where you missed attaching the right Security Group to the instance:

    1. Log in to the **AWS Console** | **EC2** | **Instances**.

    2. Select **Instance** | **Security Group**.

| Instance: i-0bcab82c096b2e060 (Ansible) | Elastic IP: 34.231.93.46 |
|---|---|

| Description | Status Checks | Monitoring | Tags | Usage Instructions |
|---|---|---|---|---|

| | | |
|---|---|---|
| Instance ID | i-0bcab82c096b2e060 | Public DNS (IPv4 |
| Instance state | running | IPv4 Public I |
| Instance type | t2.micro | IPv6 IP |
| Elastic IPs | 34.231.93.46* | Private DN |
| Availability zone | us-east-1a | Private IP |
| Security groups | Ansible-Controller-SG . view inbound rules | Secondary private IP |
| Scheduled events | No scheduled events | VPC I |
| AMI ID | CentOS Linux 7 x86_64 HVM EBS 1704_01-b7ee8a69-ee97-4a49-9e68-afaee216db2e-ami-d52f5bc3.4 (ami-46c1b650) | Subnet I |

Check Security Group

3.  Select the **Inbound** tab.

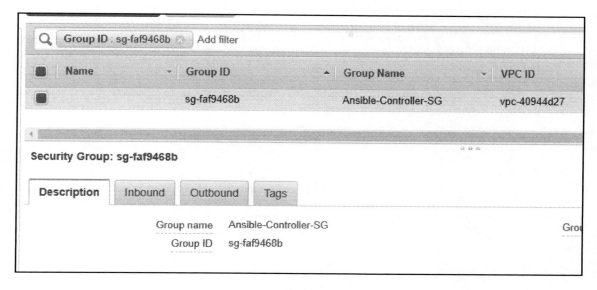

Select Security Group

4.  Your Security Group should allow SSH access over port 22 from your IP.

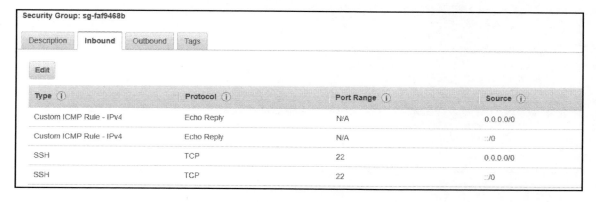

| Type | Protocol | Port Range | Source |
|---|---|---|---|
| Custom ICMP Rule - IPv4 | Echo Reply | N/A | 0.0.0.0/0 |
| Custom ICMP Rule - IPv4 | Echo Reply | N/A | ::/0 |
| SSH | TCP | 22 | 0.0.0.0/0 |
| SSH | TCP | 22 | ::/0 |

Check Inbound Rules

1. If SSH access is not available, create a new rule by clicking on **Edit | Add Rule.**

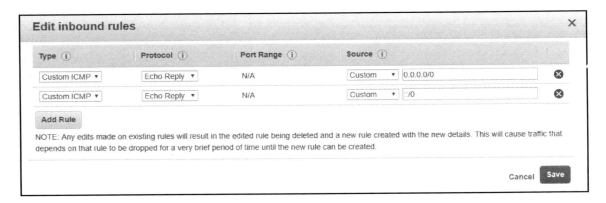

Add Inbound Rule in Security Group

2. Select **Type | SSH | Source | My IP** and click on **Save.**

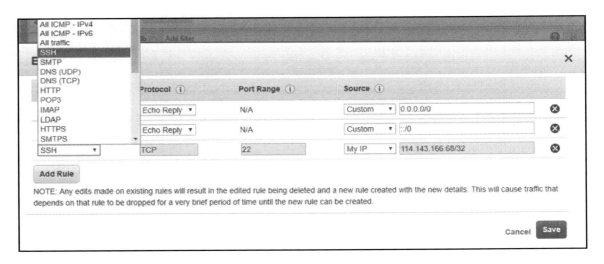

Security Group: Add SSH Rule

5. Check whether the server has been created in the right subnet or whether the subnet allows traffic from the necessary ports and protocols.

1. Log in to the **AWS Console** | **Amazon Virtual Private Cloud (VPC)** and navigate to Network ACLs.
2. Choose either the **Inbound Rules** or **Outbound Rules** tab.
3. Choose to **Allow for the traffic** from the source IP address in both inbound and outbound rules.

# There's more...

If you still face this issue when connecting instances, there could be multiple reasons. The reasons can be as follows:

- Local firewall rules
- Routing policy of your network
- Trying to connect with the wrong key pair

# Internet not accessible in the instance

You are connected to your public subnet instance but, while updating the OS or trying to connect to the internet, you get an error. In this recipe, we will look at the possible reasons for internet related issues.

We will discuss private instances in a later section.

# Getting ready

For troubleshooting, you will need access to the server and the VPC.

# How to do it...

1. Verify whether the Route Table has the appropriate routes entered for the destination `0.0.0.0/0` via the Internet Gateway.
   1. Log in to the **AWS Console** | **Amazon Virtual Private Cloud (VPC)**.
   2. Select **Route Tables** from the navigation pane.

3. Choose the Route Table associated with your subnet instance.

Select Route Table

4. Select the **Routes** tab. Check whether the default routes (as mentioned in the image) are attached or any customized route is available to the instance.

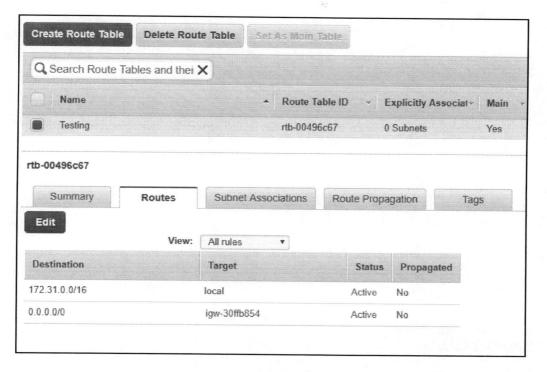

Check Routes

2. Check whether the Internet Gateway is attached to the VPC:
    1. Log in to the AWS Console and select **Amazon Virtual Private Cloud (VPC)**.

2. Navigate to **Internet Gateways** and choose **Create Internet Gateway**.

Goto Internet Gateway

3. Select the Internet Gateway and check whether it is connected to the right VPC.

Select Internet Gateway

4. If not attached, Choose **Attach to VPC**, and select your VPC from the list.

# There's more...

There can be various other reasons, which are as follows:

- OS firewall rules or SELinux
- Confirm DNS Resolution

# Internet not accessible in the private subnet instance (NAT Gateway)

While working with a private instance, we face various issues in terms of an EC2 instance connecting to the internet or any other instance in the subnet.

# How to do it...

1. The first troubleshooting step starts with pinging the destination (any other host or internet).

 Make sure that you test the destination from another server or your own computer because the destination host/website should have ICMP enabled.

2. Verify that NAT Gateway and EC2 are attached to the desired subnet.
3. Ensure that NAT Gateway has been created in a public subnet.

 Public subnet should have a public Route Table having a default route pointing to the Internet Gateway.

4. Check that the NAT Gateway is in an **available** state. If the NAT Gateway goes into a **failed** state, you will need to resolve the issue or create a new one immediately.

A failed NAT Gateway will be deleted automatically at some time, usually in an hour.

5. Make sure you don't have any blocked rules in the Network ACLs associated with your VPC.

6. Ensure that the security group rules for your private instance allows outbound internet traffic. For the `ping` command to work, the rules must also allow outbound ICMP traffic.

# Not able to delete a VPC

Now you have created a VPC, but you are unable to delete it.

## Getting ready

Before deleting a VPC, all the resources attached to the VPC have to be terminated or released.

## How to do it...

1. Check whether the NAT gateway is detached.
2. Disassociate the Elastic IP.
3. Remove dependencies between security groups
4. Terminate the EC2 instance.
5. Terminate the RDS instance and the DB subnet group.
6. Delete the Virtual Private Gateway.
7. All the VPN attachments will be terminated.
8. Delete the Internet Gateway.
9. Delete the Route Tables.

# Enabling VPC flow logs

VPC flow logs is a feature which helps in capturing information about the IP network traffic going to and from the VPC. This information can be used for troubleshooting connectivity and security. All the logs are stored in CloudWatch logs. You can also trigger an alarm for certain use cases or threats.

## Getting ready

You will need access to the VPC and CloudWatch.

## How to do it...

1. Log in to the **AWS Console** and then select **VPC**.
   1. Select your VPC | **Actions** | **Create Flow Log**.

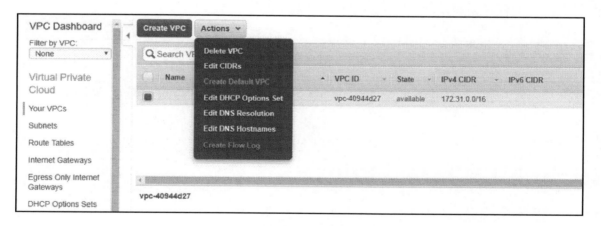

Create Flow Log

2. Click **Create Flow Log**.

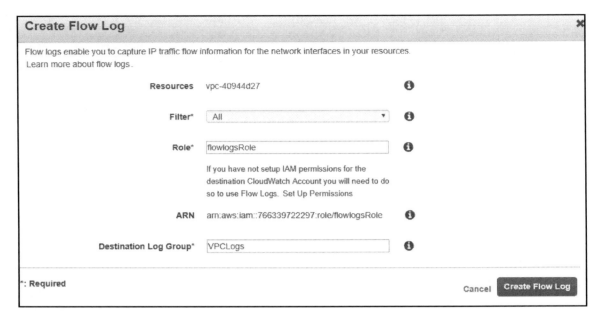

Create Flow Log

3. Create a role if it's not already there by selecting **Set Up Permissions**.

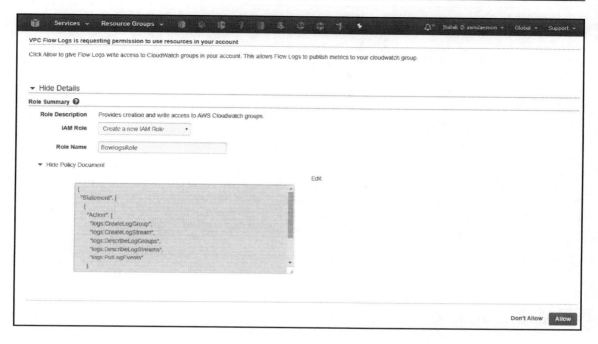

Create Flow Log

4. Navigate to **Flow Logs** in the lower pane.

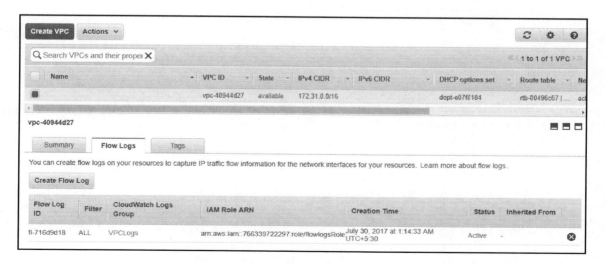

Navigate Flow Log

5. **Flow Logs** will appear in the **Cloudwatch Logs**.

Check Flow Log in CloudWatch

# There's more...

- Flow logs will not include the following traffic:
    - VPC flow logs support network interfaces created in VPC only, that is, EC2-classic links are not supported.
    - Traffic to or from DNS servers.
    - Windows license activation traffic.
    - Traffic to and from instance metadata (that is, `169.254.169.254`) requests.
    - DHCP requests or responses.
- Flow logs cannot be tagged
- Flow logs configurations can't be changed once created, so you need to delete the existing ones and create new ones.

# Increasing VPC Limits

VPC and, in fact, all AWS resources come with certain soft/hard limits so that people don't misuse or continue to spin up instances without any requirement. It also helps if your AWS server/account gets hacked and the hacker starts spinning up multiple high configuration servers to give you a billing heart attack.

# Getting ready

Limits of various services:

| Sr.no | Resources | Default limit | Limit type | Comments |
|---|---|---|---|---|
| 1 | VPC per region | 5 | Soft Limit | Internet Gateway per region will also increase by the same number |
| 2 | Subnets per VPC | 200 | Soft Limit | |
| 3 | EIP per region | 5 | Soft Limit | This limit is for VPC specific resources apart from EC2 |
| 4 | Flow logs per ENI per region | 2 | Hard Limit | |
| 5 | Customer Gateway per region | 50 | Soft Limit | |
| 6 | Internet Gateway per region | 5 | Soft Limit | This is directly related to VPCs and cannot be increased without increasing the VPC |
| 7 | NAT Gateway per AZ | 5 | Soft Limit | |
| 8 | Virtual private gateway per region | 5 | Soft Limit | |
| 9 | NACL per VPC | 200 | Hard Limit | Single NACL can be attached to multiple subnets |
| 10 | Rules per NACL | 20 | Soft Limit | This can be increased to 40 |
| 11 | ENI per region | 350 | Soft Limit | *No of ENI = No. of Instance * 5* |
| 12 | Route Tables per VPC | 200 | Soft Limit | |
| 13 | Routes per Route Table (Propagated Routes) | 100 | Hard Limit | |
| 14 | Routes per Route Table (Non Propagated Routes) | 50 | Soft Limit | Max Limit = 100 |

| 15 | Security Groups per VPC | 500 | Soft Limit | |
| 16 | Inbound/outbound rules per vpc | 50 | Soft Limit | *50 inbound + 50 outbound (Total Max = 250)* |
| 17 | Security Groups per ENI | 5 | Soft Limit | Max Limit = 16 |
| 18 | VPC Peering connections per VPC | 50 | Soft Limit | Max Limit = 125 |
| 19 | Outstanding VPC peering connection requests | 25 | Soft Limit | |
| 20 | VPC endpoint per region | 20 | Soft Limit | Max Limit = 255 endpoints |
| 21 | VPN connections per VPC | 50 | Soft Limit | |
| 22 | VPN connections per region | 10 | Soft Limit | |

# How to do it...

Follow the below steps to increase the limit of any resource:

1. Log in to the **AWS Console** and click on **Support** (Upper right-hand side corner).

Navigate Support Center

2. Click **Create Case**.

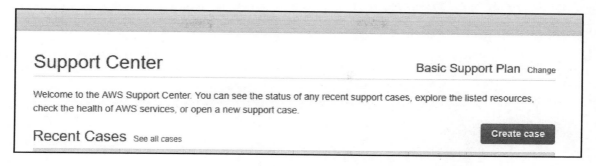

Create Support case

3. Select **Regarding** as **Service Limit Increase** and **Limit Type** as EC2 instances (or any other service you want to increase the limit for).

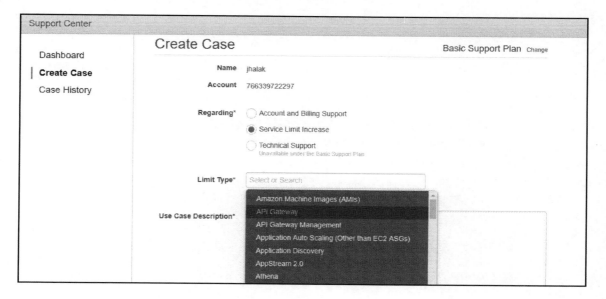

Provide Support Case Details

4. Provide the required details as asked for in the form. You can also add another request within the same ticket.

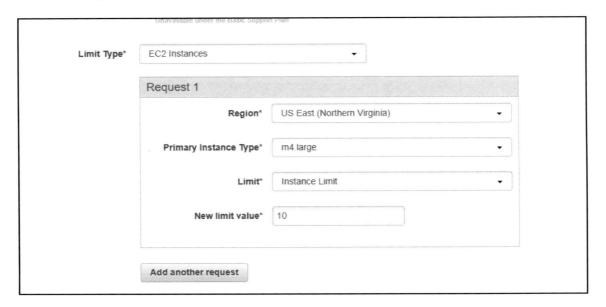

Provide New limit details

5. Provide **Use Case Description**, **Support Language**, and **Contact method**.
6. Click on **Submit** to complete the submission.

# 9
# Pricing of VPC and Related Components

In this chapter, we shall learn the following recipes:

- VPC, VPN and Nat Gateway pricing
- EC2, ELB and Elastic IP pricing
- Route 53 pricing
- Direct Connect pricing
- CloudFront pricing
- WAF and Cloud Shield pricing

## Introduction

You have learned different recipes related to different AWS networking components and infrastructure. Let's understand how pricing is done by AWS for these services. Pricing may be different for the same components over different regions. So you should consider costing in different regions before hosting your network and infrastructure in a particular AWS region. We shall use the AWS cost calculator, which is a simple user interface that lists most of the AWS services, and we can calculate the cost of all of the services that we are going to use in our AWS infrastructure for one or multiple regions. You need to remember that the cost of the networking components is calculated on their actual usage. AWS's pricing of services changes from time to time, so you should get the latest cost from the pricing page of each service. You can see the details of AWS free at: https://aws.amazon.com/free/. Here is the list of network related free services:

The list of free networking related components are:

- VPC
- Subnet
- Internet Gateway
- Security Group
- NACL
- Routing Table
- VPC Endpoint

Also supporting services like IAM, AWS CLI, and AWS CloudFormation are free. We are providing recipe to calculate pricing for some of the AWS components. You can apply same process for other AWS components as well.

# VPC, VPN and Nat Gateway pricing

VPC and most of its components are free. However we need to pay for data that we transfer in and out of these components. To understand details of pricing, browse to the link: `https://aws.amazon.com/vpc/pricing/`.

# Getting ready

We will start by short listing regions where an infrastructure can be created which may be dependent on network latency, compliance, and so on. Also you will need to determine which VPC components and how many of them you need to create.

# How to do it...

1. Browse to the AWS cost calculator `https://calculator.s3.amazonaws.com/index.html`. **US-East** is the default region selected. Choose a different region if you wish to. Choose **Amazon VPC** from the left side menu option:

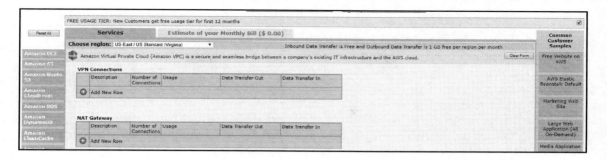

AWS cost calculator

2. Add the desired components, such as VPC, that you need to choose by clicking on **+**. If you want to delete a row, choose **-**. For the **Usage** field, you can choose the utilization % or hours or define it in terms of days or weeks or months. For each VPC, you can choose zero or more VPN connections. The cost will be updated in the **Estimate of your Monthly Bill** tab. I have added one VPC with 1 GB data in and 1 GB data out per month. You can see that the cost is zero for 100% utilization:

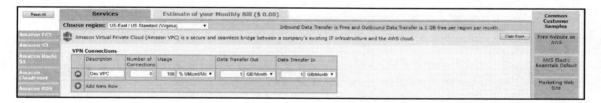

VPC cost without VPN

3. Now let's add a prod VPC with 1 VPN with 100% utilization. We can see the monthly cost has increased to **$36.60**:

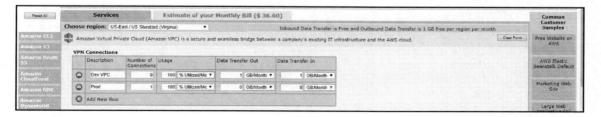

VPC cost with VPN

4. Let's add 100 GB/month data in. You can see that the cost remains the same:

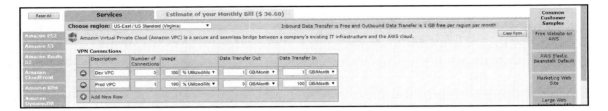

VPC cost with VPN and data in

5. Let's add 100 GB/month data transfer out. You can see that the price has increased to **$44.25**:

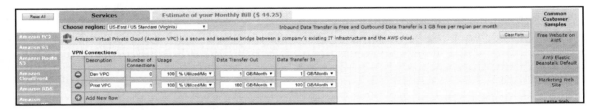

VPC cost with VPN and data in and out

6. Click on the **Estimate of Your Monthly Bill** tab. You can see the breakdown of the cost, along with the free tier discount amount:

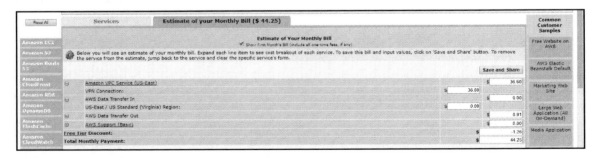

VPC cost breakdown with VPN and data in and out

7. Let's go back to the **Services** tab. Add one NAT with 100% utilization. Add 100 GB data in and out. You can see that the cost has further increased to **$90.69**:

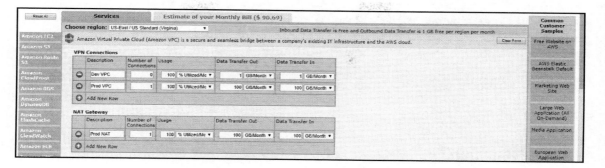

VPC cost with VPN, NAT and data in and out

8. Click on the **Estimate of Your Monthly Bill** tab. You can see the breakdown of the cost, with the NAT cost added:

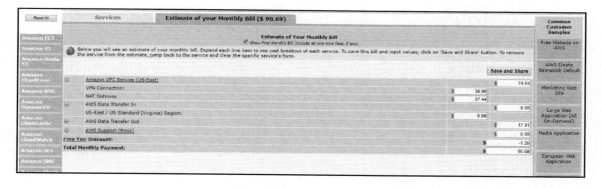

VPC cost breakup with VPN, NAT and data in and out

# There's more...

The data transfer cost is different with different usage levels. With higher usage, the cost reduces. You can see this at: `https://aws.amazon.com/ec2/pricing/on-demand/#Data_Transfer`.

# EC2, ELB and Elastic IP pricing

EC2 is the infrastructure service that you need to host your application. You need services such as EBS to be attached to EC2. Elastic IP or ELB can be used to expose your service, hosted on EC2 to the end users. The cost of EC2 is dependent on the type of EC2 and the operating system. Discounts are available for reserved instances. We should consider shared instances with on demand usage for costing. Dedicated instances are also available for special purposes. To understand details of pricing, go to `https://aws.amazon.com/ec2/pricing/`.

## Getting ready

We will start by short listing regions where an infrastructure can be created, which may be dependent on network latency, compliance, and so on. Perhaps you also need to determine how many of the EC2, EBS, ELB, and EIP components you will need to create.

## How to do it...

1. Open a new cost calculator if you want to have the cost for only EC2 related components or use the same cost calculator used for the earlier recipe. Choose **Amazon EC2** from the left menu bar:

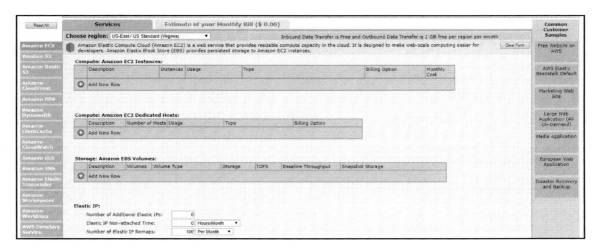

AWS cost calculator for EC2

2. Click + under **Compute: Amazon EC2 Instances:** to add EC2 to the cost calculator. Enter the description, the number of instances, and the usage details. Click on the icon for type. The following window will open. Choose the instance type and operating system based on your need. Click on **Close and Save:**

Operating System
- ○ Windows
- ○ Windows and Std. SQL Server
- ○ Windows and Web SQL Server
- ○ Windows and Enterprise SQL Server
- ● Linux
- ○ Red Hat Enterprise Linux
- ○ SUSE Linux Enterprise Server
- ☐ EBS-Optimized

| | | | | | | | | |
|---|---|---|---|---|---|---|---|---|
| ○ | m4.16xlarge | 64 | 256.0 | -- | 10 Gigabit | -- | $3.200 | $1.203 (62%) |
| ○ | m3.medium | 1 | 3.75 | SSD 1 x 4 | Moderate | -- | $0.067 | $0.026 (61%) |
| ○ | m3.large | 2 | 7.5 | SSD 1 x 32 | Moderate | -- | $0.133 | $0.052 (61%) |
| ○ | m3.xlarge | 4 | 15.0 | SSD 2 x 40 | High | Yes | $0.266 | $0.105 (61%) |
| ○ | m3.2xlarge | 8 | 30.0 | SSD 2 x 80 | High | Yes | $0.532 | $0.209 (61%) |
| ● | c4.large | 2 | 3.7 | -- | Moderate | Yes | $0.100 | $0.039 (61%) |
| ○ | c4.xlarge | 4 | 7.5 | -- | High | Yes | $0.199 | $0.078 (61%) |
| ○ | c4.2xlarge | 8 | 15.0 | -- | High | Yes | $0.398 | $0.155 (61%) |
| ○ | c4.4xlarge | 16 | 30.0 | -- | High | Yes | $0.796 | $0.310 (61%) |
| ○ | c4.8xlarge | 36 | 60.0 | -- | 10 Gigabit | Yes | $1.591 | $0.621 (61%) |
| ○ | c3.large | 2 | 3.7 | SSD 2 x 16 | Moderate | -- | $0.105 | $0.039 (63%) |
| ○ | c3.xlarge | 4 | 7.5 | SSD 2 x 40 | Moderate | Yes | $0.210 | $0.079 (62%) |
| ○ | c3.2xlarge | 8 | 15.0 | SSD 2 x 80 | High | Yes | $0.420 | $0.157 (63%) |
| ○ | c3.4xlarge | 16 | 30.0 | SSD 2 x 160 | High | Yes | $0.840 | $0.315 (63%) |
| ○ | c3.8xlarge | 32 | 60.0 | SSD 2 x 320 | 10 Gigabit | -- | $1.680 | $0.628 (63%) |
| ○ | p2.xlarge | 4 | 61.0 | -- | High | -- | $0.900 | $0.399 (56%) |
| ○ | p2.8xlarge | 32 | 488.0 | -- | 10 Gigabit | -- | $7.200 | $3.196 (56%) |

Advanced Options
[ Show ]

* assumes 100% usage and Reserved Instance paid all upfront (more billing options available)

[ Close ] [ Close and Save ]

EC2 OS and instance type selection

3. Click the icon next to the billing options. The following window will open.
Choose the required billing option and click on **Close and Save**. For reserved
options, you may pay upfront, partially upfront or no upfront fee at all. You need
to make the upfront payment at the start of your reservation, as shown in
the **Upfront Price** column. **Effective Hourly Cost** shows the per hour charge for
using the instance:

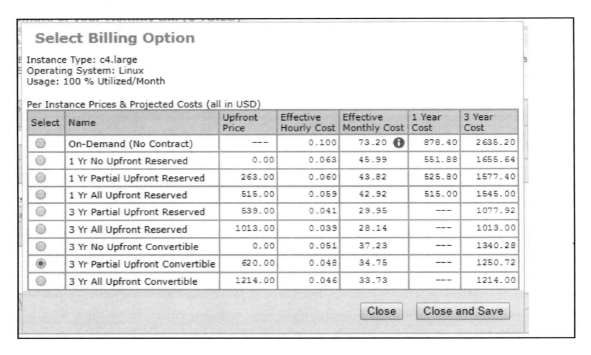

EC2 pricing options

4. Now let's add the cost of storage attached to the EC2 instance. Click + under
**Storage: Amazon EBS Volumes:**. Add the volume description, the number of
volumes, the volume type, the storage amount and the snapshot size for backup:

EBS pricing options

5. Next, add the Elastic IP requirement details and data transfer details:

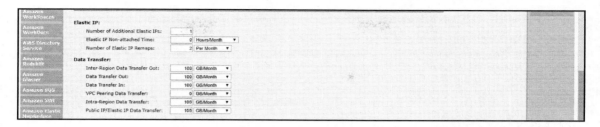

Elastic IP and data transfer options

6. Finally, add ELB and the data processed by ELB:

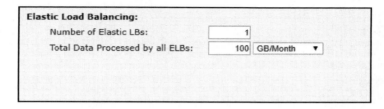

Load balancing options

7. Browse to the **Estimate of Your Monthly Bill** tab. You will be able to see the details for the cost components:

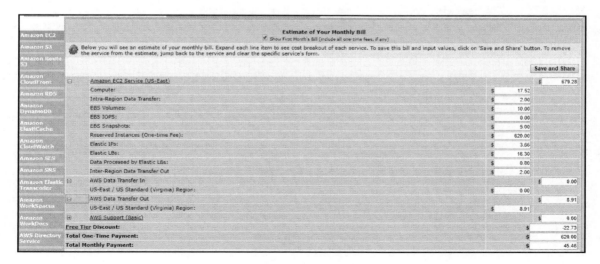

Monthly bill for EC2

# Route 53 pricing

Route 53 is priced for pay per use DNS service. It has components such as hosted zones, traffic flow and queries. AWS has a staggering price for the number of hosted zones and queries, with a lesser unit price beyond a certain usage. For details, check `https://aws.amazon.com/route53/pricing/`.

## Getting ready

You need to decide the amount of traffic flow, the hosted zones and the health check to be used for Route 53.

## How to do it...

1. Open a new cost calculator if you want to have the cost for only Route 53 related components or use the same cost calculator used for earlier recipes. Choose **Amazon Route 53** from the left menu bar:

AWS cost calculator for Route 53

2. Add the hosted zones, the traffic flow and type and the number of queries. You can see the estimated bill on the other tab:

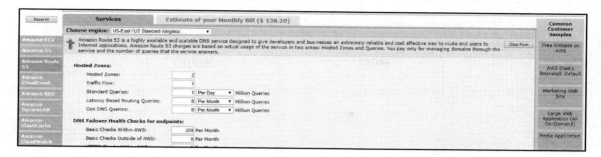

Route 53 cost for Hosted zone components

3. Add DNS failover details under **DNS Failover Health Checks for endpoints**:

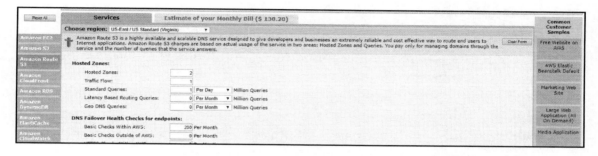

Route 53 cost for Hosted zone components and Failover health check

4. Browse to the **Estimate of your Monthly Bill** tab. You will be able to see the details for the cost components:

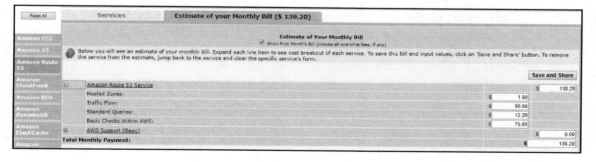

Route 53 monthly bill

# Direct Connect pricing

Direct Connect comes with a dedicated bandwidth connectivity ranging from 50 MB per second to 10 GB per second. It also has certain locations to which you need to establish connectivity for your data center.

## Getting ready

We first need to finalize the number and bandwidth connectivity for Direct Connect.

## How to do it...

1. Open a new cost calculator if you only want to have the cost for Direct Connect related components, or use the same cost calculator used for earlier recipes. Choose **AWS Direct Connect** from the left menu bar:

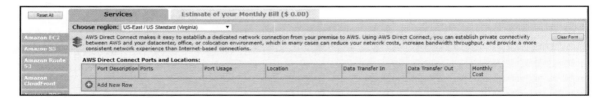

AWS cost calculator for Direct Connect

2. Add Direct Connect by clicking on **+**. If you want to delete a row, choose **-**. Provide the **Port Description**, number of ports and width, **Port Usage**, and **Location**. There are many locations available nearest to the AWS region, as shown in the following screenshot:

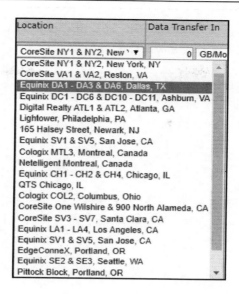

Direct Connect locations

3. Put in values for **Data Transfer In** and **Data Transfer Out** and get the final pricing:

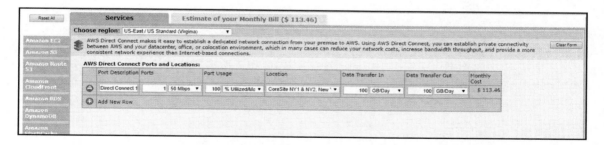

Direct Connect cost components

4. Browse to the **Estimate of your Monthly Bill** tab. You will be able to see the details for the cost components:

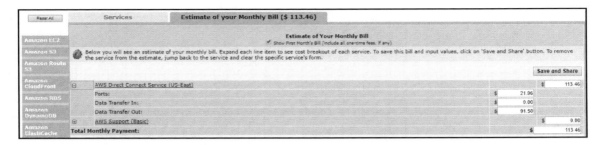

Direct Connect monthly bill

# CloudFront pricing

**CloudFront** is a caching service provided by AWS. There is a certain free use limit for CloudFront. The AWS CloudFront price is different for different geographic regions. You can get a discount for reserved pricing if you commit certain uses for at least 12 months. For details go to: `https://aws.amazon.com/cloudfront/pricing/`.

# Getting ready

We first need to finalize the data transfer amount, the request type, and the request.

# How to do it...

1. Open a new cost calculator if you want to have the cost for only CloudFront related components, or use the same cost calculator used for earlier recipes. Choose **AWS CloudFront** from the left menu bar:

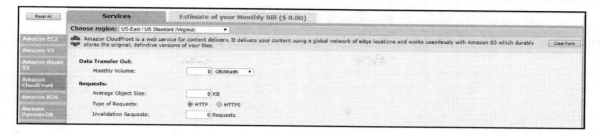

AWS cost calculator for CloudFront

2. Provide the data transfer volume, the average object size and the invalidation requests:

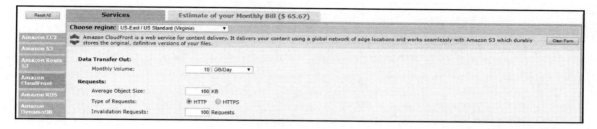

CloudFront data transfer and request

3. Provide the traffic distribution over the world, if you know. Provide the IP SSL certificates for HTTPS requests:

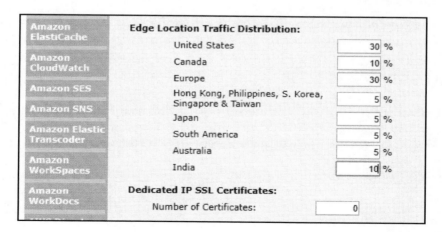

CloudFront data distribution

4. Browse to the **Estimate of your Monthly Bill** tab. You will be able to see the details for the cost components:

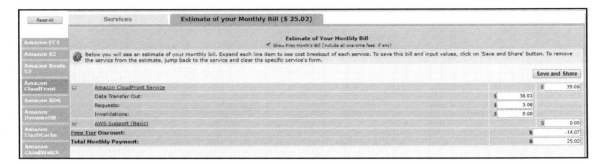

CloudFront monthly bill

# WAF and Cloud Shield pricing

WAF and Cloud Shield pricing is still not integrated with the AWS cost calculator. Let's understand their pricing model. WAF can be integrated with ELB and CloudFront, so the WAF bill is included in the CloudFront or the ELB with which it is integrated.

## Getting ready

We first need to understand the components of the services.

## How to do it...

1. Go to https://aws.amazon.com/waf/pricing/. You can see that the WAF price is based on the number of web ACL and rules. For example, if you have 2 web ACLs and 20 rules, the cost per month will be as follows:

   *(2 * $5 per web ACL per month) + (20 * $1 per rule per web ACL per month) = $30*

2. WAF has an additional price for the number of requests. For example, if your application receives 20 million requests, then the cost per month will be:

   *20*$0.60 per million web requests = $12*

3. So the total cost of WAF is $42 per month.
4. AWS Cloud Shield is free and is integrated with **Elastic Load Balancing (ELB)**, Application Load Balancer, Amazon CloudFront, and Amazon Route 53. You don't need to pay anything extra for the AWS Cloud Shield.
5. However, there is another option, AWS Shield Advanced which needs one year's commitment and comes with a monthly fee of $3000. It has additional costs for data transfers, as well as for Application Load Balancer and Amazon CloudFront. The data transfer price is different for each of these services and is priced as pay per use. The cost is different at different usage levels. For details, check `https://aws.amazon.com/shield/pricing/`.
6. If you use the AWS Cloud Shield Advanced, and your application needs to transfer 500 GB of data out, cost per month will be as follows:

   *3000 + 500* Data Transfer Out Price (0.05 $ per GB) = $3025*

# Index

Customer Gateway (CGW) 123

# D

DC connectivity
  VPC, creating 138, 143
Direct Connect pricing 338, 340
Domain Name System (DNS) 10
Domain Name System Security Extensions
    (DNSSEC) 225
domain
  registering 219
  transferring, into Amazon Route 53 223

# E

EC2 instance
  about 332
  creating, with IPv6 address 26, 34
  errors, while connecting 306
  managing 76, 84
  NAT, creating 34
edge locations 252
Egress-Only Internet Gateway 41
Elastic IP pricing
  about 332
  URL 332
Elastic Load Balancer (ELB)
  about 332, 343
  application, creating 99, 104
  setting up 279
Elastic Network Interface (ENI)
  about 41, 86
  multiple IPs, assigning 86, 89
error responses
  customizing, in CloudFront 269, 271

# F

failover routing policy
  working with 241, 247

# G

geographic restrictions
  with Amazon CloudFront 266, 269

# H

health checks
  working with 241, 246
hosted zones
  creating 225

# I

Identity and Access Management (IAM)
  URL 19
Infrastructure as a Service (IaaS)
  about 168, 250
  automation tools 170
  automation, need for 169
instances
  accessing, outside AWS 95, 99
  accessing, within network 89, 95
  internet accessibility, avoiding 313
  multiple IPs, assigning 86, 89
Internet Gateway
  about 10
  managing 64, 67
Internet Protocol (IP) 60
IP address overlapping
  troubleshooting 306
IPv6 address
  EC2, creating 26, 34
IPv6
  migrating to 160, 166
  VPC, creating 22, 26

# L

launch configuration
  creating 104
log Information
  protecting 286, 295

# M

multi-factor authentication (MFA) 19
multi-region VPC communication
  creating 147, 154

# N

Nat Gateway pricing
  about 328

URL 328, 331
NAT Gateway
  managing 68, 71
Network Access Control List (NACL)
  about 10
  managing 55, 60
Network Address Translation (NAT)
  about 67
  creating, on EC2 instance 34, 41
network interfaces
  working with 41, 44

# P

penetration testing request
  submitting 300
Platform as a Service (PaaS) 10, 250
points of presence (POP) 252
private DNS
  setting up, with VPC 155, 160
private hosted zone
  creating 233
private subnet instance
  internet accessibility, avoiding 317
private subnets
  about 67
  managing 52, 54
  VPC, creating 144, 146
public cloud computing 9
public hosted zone
  deleting 229, 231
public subnets
  about 67
  managing 52, 54

# R

Real-Time Messaging Protocol (RTMP) 252
record sets
  creating 225
Remote Desktop Protocol (RDP) 95
Route 53 pricing
  about 336
  URL 336
Route 53
  about 215
  alias resource record 218

DNS, working 216
domain, transferring into 223
routing policies 218
supported DNS resource record types 217
used, for registering domain 219
Route Table
  about 10
  managing 71, 76
Router 11

# S

Security Group (SG)
  about 10
  managing 60, 64
server-side encryption (SSE) 300
Single sign on (SSO) 250
Software as a Service (SAAS) 250
strongSwan 147
subnet
  about 10
  creating, with IPv6 22, 26

# T

time to live (TTL) 218
Trusted Advisor 279, 286

# U

US-Standard 263

# V

Virtual Private Gateway (VGW) 11, 123
Virtual Routing and Forwarding (VRF) 10
VPC flow logs
  enabling 319
VPC peering
  accepting 119, 122
  access, controlling 123
  connection, limitations 123
  creating 117, 118
  routes, configuring 122
VPC
  about 328
  creating, from CLI 134
  creating, to DC connectivity 138, 143

Made in the USA
Middletown, DE
08 March 2018